The British Women's Suffrage Campaign, 1866–1928

The British Women's Suffrage Campaign, 1866–1928

Revised second edition

Harold L. Smith

Longman
is an imprint of

Harlow, England • London • New York • Boston • San Francisco • Toronto • Sydney • Singapore • Hong Kong
Tokyo • Seoul • Taipei • New Delhi • Cape Town • Madrid • Mexico City • Amsterdam • Munich • Paris • Milan

PEARSON EDUCATION LIMITED

Edinburgh Gate
Harlow CM20 2JE
United Kingdom
Tel: +44 (0)1279 623623
Fax: +44 (0)1279 431059
Website: www.pearsoned.co.uk

First edition published 1998
Second edition published in 2007
This revised second edition published in Great Britain 2010

© Pearson Education Limited 1998, 2010

The right of Harold L. Smith to be identified as author of this work has been asserted
by him in accordance with the Copyright, Designs and Patents Act 1988.

ISBN: 978-1-4082-2823-4

British Library Cataloguing in Publication Data
A catalogue record for this book is available from the British Library

Library of Congress Cataloging in Publication Data
Smith, Harold L.
  The British women's suffrage campaign, 1866–1928 / Harold L. Smith. – 2nd rev. ed.
     p. cm.
  Includes bibliographical references and index.
  ISBN 978-1-4082-2823-4 (pbk.)
  1. Women–Suffrage–Great Britain–History–19th century.   2. Women–Suffrage–Great
Britain–History–20th century.   3. Feminism–Great Britain–History.   4. Women in
politics–Great Britain–History.   I. Title.
  HQ1236.5.G7s55 2009
  324.6'230941—dc22s

                                                                          2009030700

10 9 8 7 6 5 4 3 2 1
13 12 11 10 09

Set in 10/13.5pt Berkeley by 35
Printed in Malaysia (CTP-VVP)

The Publisher's policy is to use paper manufactured from sustainable forests.

Contents

Introduction to the series

History is a narrative constructed by historians from traces left by the past. Historical enquiry is often driven by contemporary issues and, in consequence, historical narratives are constantly revisited and reshaped. *Seminar Studies in History* was designed to bridge the gap between current research and the broad, popular general surveys that often date rapidly.

The volumes in the series are written by historians who are not only familiar with the latest research in, and current debates about, their topic, but also have contributed to that research and the debates. The books are intended to provide the reader with a clear introduction to a major topic in history. They give a narrative and analysis of events and highlight contemporary controversies. They include the kinds of tools generally omitted from specialist monographs – chronologies and a glossary – as well as that essential tool, an up-to-date bibliography. They conclude with a selection of documents – some traces of the past illustrative of events described, which also serve as the historian's raw materials.

List of plates

Acknowledgements

This book is dedicated to Judy.

I would like to thank David Doughan, formerly the Fawcett Reference Librarian, for his assistance above and beyond the call of duty. Special thanks are due to Philippa Levine for reading and commenting on Chapter One. I would like to thank the University of Houston-Victoria for financial support which made a research trip to Great Britain possible. But above all, I would like to thank my life-partner and in-house editor: Judith N. McArthur.

Publisher's acknowledgements

We are grateful to the following for permission to reproduce copyright material:

Plates 1, 3, 4 and 5 courtesy of the Museum of London; plates 2, 8 and 9 courtesy of the Mary Evans Picture Library; plate 6 courtesy of the Illustrated London News Picture Library; plate 7 courtesy of Hulton Archive/Getty Images; plate 10 courtesy of the Burrell Collection, Glasgow City Council (Museums).

In some instances we have been unable to trace owners of copyright material, and would appreciate any information that would enable us to do so.

Chronology

1905   (October) Christabel Pankhurst and Annie Kenney arrested (militancy begins)

1906   Liberal Party wins the general election

        WSPU moves headquarters to London

        WSPU severs ties with ILP

1907   (February) NUWSS sponsors Mud March

        NUWSS adopts new constitution

        Men's League for Women's Suffrage formed

        Conservative and Unionist Women's Franchise Association (CUWFA) established

        WSPU begins publication of *Votes for Women*

        (September) WSPU split; dissidents expelled

        (October) Women's Freedom League (WFL) established

1908   (June) Hyde Park mass meeting

        (June) WSPU window breaking initiated

        (November) NUWSS dissociates itself from WSPU violence

        National League for Opposing Women's Suffrage established

1909   NUWSS begins publication of *Common Cause*

        People's Suffrage Federation (PSF) formed

        Church League for Women's Suffrage established

        Scottish Federation of the NUWSS formed

1910   All-party Conciliation Committee created

        (November) Black Friday

1911   Forward Cymric Suffrage Union established

        Catholic Women's Suffrage Society (CWSS) established

1912   (March) Christabel flees to Paris

        NUWSS–Labour Party alliance established

        (July) WSPU arson campaign initiated

        (October) Pethick-Lawrences expelled from the WSPU

        (November) George Lansbury defeated in by-election

1913   (January) Emily Davison's death

        (April) Temporary Discharge for Ill-Health Act [known as 'Cat and Mouse Act']

1914   (January) Sylvia Pankhurst expelled from the WSPU

        (February) United Suffragists formed

        (June) ELF deputation to Prime Minister Asquith

        (July) First World War begins

1915   (February–March) NUWSS split

(May) NUWSS suspends Election Fighting Fund (EFF) policy

(October) British section of the Women's International League formed

1916   (March) Consultative Committee of Constitutional Women's Suffrage Societies formed

(March) The Independent WSPU established

The Suffragettes of the WSPU formed

Speaker's Conference on electoral reform appointed

(August) Consultative Committee's recommendations sent to the Prime Minister

(September) National Council for Adult Suffrage established

1917   (January) Speaker's Conference recommends women's suffrage

(February) NUWSS deputation to Local Government Board (LGB) pledges to support the Speaker's Report

(26 March) Cabinet agrees to proceed with the franchise reform bill

(28 March) House of Commons votes for the reform bill

(29 March) Suffrage societies' deputation to the Prime Minister

(19 June) House of Commons votes for the women's suffrage clause in reform bill

1918   Representation of the People Act extends the vote to women aged 30 and above who were also local electors or the wives of local government electors

1919   Women's Emancipation Bill debated in Parliament

1921   (February) Six Point Group established

(March) Consultative Committee of Women's Organisations formed

1924   Baldwin declares Conservative Party supports equal political rights

1925   (February) Joynson Hicks pledges equal franchise before the next election

1926   (July) Hyde Park mass meeting for equal franchise

1927   (12 April) Cabinet agrees to equal suffrage legislation

1928   Representation of the People (Equal Franchise) Act enfranchises women aged 21 and over

Who's who

Astor, Nancy (1879–1964): In 1919 Astor became the first female member of the House of Commons. She established the Consultative Committee of Women's Organisations in 1921 to develop an agreed feminist reform programme. Astor was the key female within the Conservative Party lobbying for equal franchise in the 1920s.

Becker, Lydia (1827–1890): After serving as secretary of the Manchester Society for Women's Suffrage, Becker became the first secretary of the National Society for Women's Suffrage. She remained its leader and edited the *Women's Suffrage Journal* until the late 1880s.

Billington-Greig, Teresa (1877–1964): An ILP organizer who also became one of the WSPU's first organizers. She was one of the leaders of the revolt against the Pankhursts when they broke with the ILP, and became a leader of the Women's Freedom League.

Despard, Charlotte (1844–1939): A WSPU member who withdrew when it broke with the ILP. One of the founders of the Women's Freedom League, she became its first President.

Fawcett, Millicent Garrett (1847–1929): Fawcett became a member of the London Society for Women's Suffrage's executive when it was formed in 1867 and was the leader of the NUWSS from its formation in 1897. Although reluctant to publicly criticize WSPU militant methods, she insisted the NUWSS rely on constitutional methods and privately believed WSPU militancy after 1910 was undermining the NUWSS's efforts to win converts to the suffrage cause.

Marshall, Catherine (1880–1961): Marshall was an important leader of the 'democratic suffragists' within the NUWSS. She became the NUWSS's Parliamentary secretary in 1911 and was appointed secretary of the Election Fighting Fund Committee when it was established in 1912.

Pankhurst, Christabel (1880–1958): Emmeline Pankhurst's eldest daughter. One of the earliest WSPU members, she introduced militant methods into the WSPU suffrage campaign. After 1907 she and her mother emerged as the dominant figures within the WSPU.

Pankhurst, Emmeline (1858–1928): Founded the WSPU in 1903 and always its spiritual leader although her daughter Christabel assumed greater responsibility for directing the WSPU campaign after 1910. Repeatedly imprisoned during the suffrage campaign, she inspired many women to join the suffrage movement by her willingness to sacrifice her life if necessary for the cause.

Pankhurst, Sylvia (1882–1960): Emmeline Pankurst's daughter. Although she remained in the WSPU when her mother and her sister Christabel broke with the ILP, she disagreed with their policy and sought to link feminism and socialism. Expelled from the WSPU by Christabel in 1914, she formed her own organization, the East London Federation of the Women's Social and Political Union.

Rathbone, Eleanor (1872–1946): Rathbone became the Liverpool Women's Suffrage Society's secretary in 1897, and later became a member of the NUWSS executive. Elected President of the NUSEC in 1919, Rathbone directed the campaign for equal franchise in the 1920s.

Rhondda, Viscountess [Margaret Haig Thomas] (1883–1958): A member of the Women's Social and Political Union who was imprisoned briefly for setting fire to letterboxes. In 1921 she founded the Six Point Group to work for feminist reforms. Dissatisfied with the lack of progress towards equal franchise, she formed the Equal Political Rights Campaign Committee in 1926 in an attempt to ginger up the campaign.

Roper, Esther (1868–1938): Roper was secretary of the Manchester National Society for Women's Suffrage (later the North of England Society for Women's Suffrage) from 1893 to 1905. She was responsible for recruiting working-class women into the suffrage movement at a time when its members were mainly middle- and upper-class women.

Glossary of organisations

Catholic Women's Suffrage Society: Established in 1911 and open to Catholics of both sexes who supported women's parliamentary suffrage. After 1918 it became St Joan's Social and Political Alliance.

Conservative and Unionist Women's Franchise Association: Established in 1907 with Lady Selborne as president. Comprising Conservative Party women, it attempted to convert Conservatives to the suffrage cause.

East London Federation of the Women's Social and Political Union: Established in 1912 by Sylvia Pankhurst. When Sylvia refused to accept Christabel Pankhurst's anti-male policy, she was expelled from the WSPU and in 1914 the organization changed its name to the East London Federation of the Suffragettes.

Election Fighting Fund Committee: Established by the NUWSS in 1912 to implement the NUWSS's electoral alliance with the Labour Party. Its formation represented a triumph for the NUWSS leaders from the north of England who wished the NUWSS to become part of a more radical, democratic suffragist movement. Catherine Marshall, a leading proponent within the NUWSS of closer ties with the Labour Party, became secretary of the committee.

Equal Political Rights Demonstration Committee: An umbrella organization established in 1926 with Lady Rhondda as its leader. Dissatisfied with the lack of progress towards equal franchise, Rhondda believed more militant tactics were needed. After sponsoring a mass demonstration in July 1926, the committee changed its name to the Equal Political Rights Campaign Committee.

London Society for Women's Service: Chaired by Clementia Taylor, the London National Society for Women's Suffrage was established in 1867. After several name changes it was renamed the London Society for Women's Suffrage in 1907 and became the London Society for Women's Service in 1919. In 1953 it became the Fawcett Society.

National Society for Women's Suffrage: Established in 1867 by representatives of the London National Society for Women's Suffrage and the Manchester National Society for Women's Suffrage following the defeat of the women's suffrage amendment to the 1867 Reform Bill. It was a loose federation intended to coordinate the efforts of the regional suffrage societies. Lydia Becker, the Manchester Society's secretary, became its secretary.

National Union of Societies for Equal Citizenship: The National Union of Women's Suffrage Societies changed its name to the National Union of Societies for Equal Citizenship in 1919 to reflect its expanded reform programme. Eleanor Rathbone was its president from 1919 to 1928. It was primarily responsible for conducting the feminist campaign for equal franchise in the 1920s.

National Union of Women's Suffrage Societies: Established in 1897. Although Millicent Fawcett was not formally elected president until 1907, she was viewed as the NUWSS's leader from its beginning. In 1909 the NUWSS began publishing its own journal, *The Common Cause*, which had a circulation of 10,000 by 1912.

North of England Society for Women's Suffrage: The new name given to the Manchester National Society for Women's Suffrage when it affiliated to the National Union of Women's Suffrage Societies in 1897. With Esther Roper as its secretary, it was especially concerned with drawing working-class women into the suffrage movement.

People's Suffrage Federation: Established in 1909 by women trade unionists and Women's Co-operative Guild members. Led by Margaret Llewelyn Davies, the WCG's secretary, it advocated adult suffrage in order that working-class women would gain the right to vote.

Standing Joint Committee of Industrial Women's Organisations: Established in February 1916 by women's organizations concerned that female workers were being used by employers to undercut male wage rates. Chaired by Mary Macarthur, National Federation of Women Workers' secretary, it included representatives from the major working-class women's organizations such as the Women's Co-operative Guild and the Women's Labour League. It became the Labour Party's Women's Advisory Committee in 1918.

Women's Freedom League: Established in 1907 by WSPU members who opposed the Pankhursts' split with the Labour movement. Charlotte Despard became its president. Its journal, *The Vote*, was issued from 1909 to 1933.

Women's Liberal Federation: Established in 1887. Although Catherine (Mrs William) Gladstone became its first president, Eva McClaren was its national organizer and the real moving spirit within the organization. Although some of its founders were the wives of Liberal MPs who thought the main function of the WLF should be to help their husbands gain election, the majority of WLF members believed it should help elect Liberals who supported women's causes, such as suffrage and temperance.

Women's National Anti-Suffrage League: Established in 1908. Although Lady Jersey chaired its executive committee, Mrs Humphrey Ward, the popular novelist, was the real driving force within the organization. It merged with the men's anti-suffrage league later in 1908 and became the National League for Opposing Women's Suffrage.

Women's Social and Political Union: Established in 1903 by Emmeline Pankhurst. It used militant methods which led its members to be called 'suffragettes' to distinguish them from the constitutional suffragists. Its journal, *Votes for Women*, reached a peak circulation of almost 40,000 in 1909–10.

Abbreviations

CSU	Cymric Suffrage Union
CUWFA	Conservative and Unionist Women's Franchise Association
CWSS	Catholic Women's Suffrage Society
EFF	Election Fighting Fund Committee
ELF	East London Federation of the Women's Social and Political Union (later of the Suffragettes)
EPRDC	Equal Political Rights Demonstration Committee
ILP	Independent Labour Party
IWSA	International Women's Suffrage Alliance
LGB	Local Government Board
LNA	Ladies' National Association for the Repeal of the Contagious Diseases Acts
LNSWS	London and National Society for Women's Service
LSWS	London Society for Women's Suffrage (later London and National Society for Women's Service)
NEC	National Executive Committee (of the Labour Party)
NESWS	North of England Society for Women's Suffrage
NSWS	National Society for Women's Suffrage
NUSEC	National Union of Societies for Equal Citizenship
NUWSS	National Union of Women's Suffrage Societies
PSF	People's Suffrage Federation
SJCIWO	Standing Joint Committee of Industrial Women's Organizations
SPG	Six Point Group
UPS	Union of Practical Suffragists
US	United Suffragists
WCG	Women's Co-operative Guild
WFL	Women's Freedom League
WIL	Women's International League
WLF	Women's Liberal Federation
WLL	Women's Labour League
WNAL	Women's National Anti-Suffrage League
WSPU	Women's Social and Political Union

Part 1

BACKGROUND

1

Introduction

In terms of its stated objective, the women's suffrage campaign was a success story: the principle of women's suffrage was conceded in 1918, and equal franchise rights followed in 1928. The campaign brought into being Britain's largest women's movement, and heightened expectations of gender reform. But from the beginning of the campaign, many women had wanted something more than equal access to a male-controlled political system; they wished to change the system to reflect women's values. Although the first stage of suffrage reform was followed by a surge of legislation that women's groups had sought, by 1928 it had become apparent that this vision of a radical transformation of gender structures would not be achieved in the near future (Smith in Smith, 1990). While equal franchise provided women the opportunity to participate, parliamentary politics remained a male-dominated political system. This book attempts to explain how the women's movement succeeded in gaining suffrage reform, but was only partially successful in its efforts to eradicate broader gender barriers.

Ray Strachey's study, *The Cause* (1928), was the first serious attempt to write the history of the women's suffrage campaign, but its Whiggish account of the inevitable triumph of a just cause did not capture the public imagination (nor that of the historians) to the extent that **Sylvia Pankhurst's** *The Suffragette Movement* did when it appeared in 1931. Pankhurst's book did more than any other volume to shape interpretations of the suffrage campaign for the next 40 years: the **Women's Social and Political Union** (WSPU) was at the centre of the story and the Pankhurst women were the central characters. When the BBC prepared a documentary on the women's suffrage campaign in the 1970s, it (and the accompanying book, *Shoulder to Shoulder* by Midge Mackenzie) concentrated on the WSPU and the Pankhursts.

While the public remains fascinated by the Pankhursts, the suffrage movement's historiography has undergone a dramatic transformation during the past two decades. The publication of Sandra Holton's *Feminism and*

Pankhurst, Sylvia (1882–1960): Emmeline Pankhurst's daughter. Although she remained in the WSPU when her mother and her sister Christabel broke with the ILP, she disagreed with their policy and sought to link feminism and socialism. Expelled from the WSPU by Christabel in 1914, she formed her own organization, the East London Federation of the Women's Social and Political Union.

Women's Social and Political Union: Established in 1903 by Emmeline Pankhurst. It used militant methods which led its members to be called 'suffragettes' to distinguish them from the constitutional suffragists. Its journal, *Votes for Women*, reached a peak circulation of almost 40,000 in 1909–10.

National Union of Women's Suffrage Societies: Established in 1897. Although Millicent Fawcett was not formally elected president until 1907, she was viewed as the NUWSS's leader from its beginning. In 1909 the NUWSS began publishing its own journal, *The Common Cause*, which had a circulation of 10,000 by 1912.

Pankhurst, Emmeline: (1858–1928): Founded the WSPU in 1903 and always its spiritual leader although her daughter Christabel assumed greater responsibility for directing the WSPU campaign after 1910. Repeatedly imprisoned during the suffrage campaign, she inspired many women to join the suffrage movement by her willingness to sacrifice her life if necessary for the cause.

Rathbone, Eleanor: (1872–1946): Rathbone became the Liverpool Women's Suffrage Society's secretary in 1897, and later became a member of the NUWSS executive. Elected President of the NUSEC in 1919, Rathbone directed the campaign for equal franchise in the 1920s.

National Union of Societies for Equal Citizenship: The National Union of Women's Suffrage Societies changed its name to the National Union of Societies for Equal Citizenship in 1919 to reflect its expanded reform programme. Eleanor Rathbone was its president from 1919 to 1928. It was primarily responsible for conducting the feminist campaign for equal franchise in the 1920s.

Democracy: Women's Suffrage and Reform Politics in Britain 1900–1918 in 1986 was a turning-point. The use of new archival material by Holton, Jo Vellacott (1993), and David Rubinstein (1991) significantly altered our understanding of the **National Union of Women's Suffrage Societies** (NUWSS) and its contributions to franchise reform. Scholarly attention shifted to the innovative strategy of the NUWSS in allying with the Labour Party as the key to gaining suffrage reform, and away from the heroism of individual suffragettes.

While scholarly work on the British women's suffrage campaign was already reviving when this book's first edition was completed in 1997, that was only a prelude to the flowering of research that occurred during the following decade. Since 1997 historians have provided (to mention only a sample of the important new work): two full-length biographies of **Emmeline Pankhurst** (Purvis, 2002; Bartley, 2002); a collective biography of the Pankhursts (Pugh, 2001); a perceptive analysis of the suffrage campaign's political context to 1914 (Pugh, 2000); an impressively researched study of **Eleanor Rathbone** that sheds new light on both the NUWSS and its successor, the **National Union of Societies for Equal Citizenship** (NUSEC) (Pedersen, 2004); significant studies of the regions demonstrating the importance of the campaign outside London (Cowman, 2004; Liddington, 2006; Crawford, 2005b; Hannam in Purvis and Holton, 2000); and two important studies of the suffrage issue during the First World War (Gullace, 2002; Grayzel, 1999). Several important collections of essays have also contributed to the reassessment of the suffrage movement (see the Guide to Further Reading), as well as Elizabeth Crawford's impressively detailed encyclopedia of the suffrage campaign (Crawford, 1999), and a steady stream of articles, especially in the *Women's History Review*.

This new work has not merely provided us with more details about the suffrage campaign, but in several areas has challenged the old paradigm and offered a new conceptual framework. In the following pages I have attempted to provide both an overview of the various stages of the campaign and also a guide to the historiography, drawing special attention to the areas in which it has been altered by recent research. Since the history of the suffrage campaign remains hotly contested ground, I have attempted to point out the main areas of controversy at appropriate places in the text. Due to space limitations, I have had to prune rigorously and, in some instances, to delete topics that deserved inclusion. I would hope that readers will consider this volume the starting point of their investigation into the women's suffrage movement rather than the end.

Part 2

ANALYSIS

2

The Victorian Suffrage Campaign, 1866–97

The British women's suffrage campaign used to be portrayed as part of the nineteenth-century movement for a more democratic franchise which also sought to extend the suffrage to disenfranchised men. While acknowledging this connection, historians now view the campaign as part of a specifically women's protest against a gender system that disadvantaged females. Women sought the vote not only to gain equal citizenship rights, but also as a means to the political power necessary to transform gender structures. Accompanying this changed perspective has been a shift in how historians view the relationship between the suffrage campaign and other women's reform movements. While earlier studies considered the suffrage campaign to be separate from other Victorian female reform movements, it is now regarded as part of a broader reform impulse seeking to eliminate restrictions on women's educational and employment opportunities, gendered pay scales, the sexual double standard, and the legal authority husbands held over their wives (Levine, 1990).

ORIGINS

Women's suffrage became a matter of public concern during the early nineteenth-century discussion of franchise reform. In response to James Mill's claim in 1820 that there was no need to extend the suffrage to women because their fathers and husbands would protect their interests, William Thompson and Anna Wheeler presented a case for women's right to vote in *An Appeal of One Half the Human Race . . .* (Thompson and Wheeler, 1825). In the debate on the 1832 Reform Bill, Henry Hunt introduced a petition to grant the vote to unmarried women who met the bill's property requirements. Parliament responded by passing legislation which for the first time explicitly restricted the suffrage to men; the Reform Act specified that it enfranchised 'male persons'.

During the following decades there were several attempts to revive the issue. The Chartist movement included women in the 1838 People's Charter, although later versions changed the demand to adult male suffrage. In 1851 Anne Knight, a Quaker and anti-slavery campaigner, assisted Chartist women in establishing the Sheffield Female Political Association which drafted the women's suffrage petition introduced in the House of Lords later that year.

The organized women's movement originated with the group of women who met at Langham Place in London in the 1850s and 1860s. Led by Barbara Leigh Smith Bodichon and Bessie Rayner Parkes, it became an important source of proposals for gender reform in education, employment, and politics which they conveyed to a wider audience through their periodical, the *English Woman's Journal*. Members of this group established the Married Women's Property Committee in 1855 that successfully pressed for legal reform to grant married women property rights (Herstein, 1985). The *English Woman's Journal* encouraged interest in women's suffrage by printing articles on it in the 1860s. Women from the Langham Place circle were prominent in the Kensington Society, a debating group formed in 1865, which advocated women's suffrage among other reforms; it later became the London Society for Women's Suffrage (LSWS).

An organized women's suffrage movement emerged when a new reform bill became a possibility in the mid-1860s. John Stuart Mill included women's suffrage in his election programme when he was elected to Parliament in 1865. At Bodichon's request Mill agreed to introduce a women's suffrage amendment if the women's groups would prepare a petition [**Doc. 1, p. 117**]. Suffrage societies were quickly formed in London and Manchester; Mill presented their petition with 1,499 signatures to Parliament in 1866. When Disraeli's 1867 Reform Bill was considered by the House of Commons, Mill proposed substituting the term 'person' for 'man', but his amendment was rejected by a vote of 194 to 73.

During the 1860s suffragists often based their claim for the vote on the ground that qualified women had voted in the past, and that in 1850 Lord Brougham's Act specified that the term 'man' in all legislation was to be taken as including women unless it expressly excluded them. On this basis **Lydia Becker** encouraged women who met the 1867 Reform Act's property qualifications to attempt to register to vote. In November 1868 this view was rejected by the Court of Common Pleas in the *Chorlton* v. *Lings* decision, thus forcing the suffrage movement to seek legislation granting women the vote (van Wingerden, 1999).

Ray Strachey's portrayal of the Victorian suffrage campaign as a London-based movement, dominated by moderate women drawn from the social élite, has been revised by recent studies (Strachey, 1928). Sandra

Becker, Lydia (1827–1890): After serving as secretary of the Manchester Society for Women's Suffrage, Becker became the first secretary of the National Society for Women's Suffrage. She remained its leader and edited the *Women's Suffrage Journal* until the late 1880s.

Holton finds the roots of the women's suffrage movement in mid-nineteenth century northern radicalism, and stresses the continuity between it and the Edwardian militant suffrage movement. The women who initiated the women's suffrage movement tended to be religious dissenters, often Unitarian or Quaker, to have been active in radical political groups such as the Manchester-based Anti-Corn Law League or the anti-slavery movement, and to have connections with male radicals seeking a more democratic franchise (Holton, 1996).

Strachey presented the suffrage campaign as a socially conservative movement of respectable ladies by separating it from the reform efforts concerned with sexuality. Judith Walkowitz, however, considers the demand for the vote to have been fueled by women's growing outrage against the sexual double standard (Walkowitz, 1980). The 1864 Contagious Diseases Act (extended in 1866 and 1869) required women suspected by the police of being prostitutes to have a medical examination to determine if they had venereal disease. Women were outraged by this for several reasons. The Acts did not require that men be examined, thus implying that women were solely responsible for spreading venereal diseases. It deprived women of civil liberties, since a woman could be suspected of prostitution merely by walking in certain sections of a town. Finally, the legislation applied only to towns with military bases and seemed designed to protect the sexual double standard by enabling men to frequent prostitutes without fear of disease. The Acts thus seemed a blatant example of the tendency of an all-male Parliament elected solely by male voters to legislate in men's interests at women's expense.

Recent writing has also shifted attention away from the London Society to the more radical Manchester Society. The latter was established by Elizabeth Wolstenholme in 1866, prior to the formation of the London Society, and it became the dominant suffrage society in the early years of the campaign. Following the creation of suffrage societies in Edinburgh, Bristol, and Birmingham, it was the Manchester Society which in 1867 was responsible for bringing the local suffrage societies together in the **National Society for Women's Suffrage** (NSWS), a loose federation intended to facilitate joint action for reform (Holton, 1996). From 1872 until about 1885 the Manchester Society's annual income was usually two to three times greater than that of the London Society (Pugh, 2000).

Strachey's depiction of the suffrage leaders as conservatives is also misleading. Radical suffragists played key roles in the Manchester Society from the beginning. Wolstonholme, the society's first secretary, was notorious for her advanced feminism. Ursula Bright and her husband, Jacob Bright (the younger brother of John Bright), were prominent members, while Richard Pankhurst, a radical lawyer, joined shortly after it was formed. Pankhurst

National Society for Women's Suffrage: Established in 1867 by representatives of the London National Society for Women's Suffrage and the Manchester National Society for Women's Suffrage following the defeat of the women's suffrage amendment to the 1867 Reform Bill. It was a loose federation intended to coordinate the efforts of the regional suffrage societies. Lydia Becker, the Manchester Society's secretary, became its secretary.

drafted the first women's suffrage bill which Jacob Bright introduced in Parliament in 1870.

The Manchester Society's importance is also suggested by the fact that its secretary, Lydia Becker, was the suffrage campaign's first national secretary. Originally part of the Manchester Radical group, Becker was active in the campaign against the Contagious Diseases Acts in the 1860s and was a member of the Married Women's Property Committee until 1873. She founded the *Women's Suffrage Journal* in 1870, and edited it until her death in 1890. She became the NSWS's parliamentary secretary shortly after it was formed and directed the parliamentary campaign during the following decades.

The women who established the suffrage organizations in the 1860s were not political neophytes. Some had participated in the anti-slavery campaign, while others had been active in the Anti-Corn Law League. Suffragists drew upon their experience with these pressure groups in choosing to organize on a non-party basis and in relying on private members' bills which could be supported by backbenchers from all parties. While this approach had worked for pressure groups earlier in the century, the increased role of party in late-Victorian Britain made it less effective. Brian Harrison considers this strategy to have been a major reason for the failure to achieve reform prior to 1914 (Harrison, 1983).

Success in securing the vote in local elections encouraged reformers to anticipate an early concession of the parliamentary franchise. Jacob Bright's amendment to the 1869 Municipal Corporations (Franchise) Act granted women the right to vote in local elections on the same basis as men. This enfranchised unmarried women ratepayers; a married woman normally could not vote because her husband was legally the ratepayer. It set a precedent that led to women being granted the right to vote for the local school boards established by the 1870 Education Act. By 1892 there were 503,000 women eligible to vote in local elections in England, Scotland and Wales; they would have comprised at least ten per cent of the parliamentary electorate if women had been permitted to vote in national elections with the same qualifications (Pugh, 1985).

IDEOLOGY

The belief that the suffrage movement's ideology was based on liberal equal rights doctrine has been replaced by a more complex interpretation. Although some women did use equal rights language derived from liberalism, many did not. Some women rejected equal rights ideology because it implied that women wished to have the rights men did and, by implication, to become more like men. Rather than minimize sexual difference as equal rights advocates did, they celebrated difference in order to encourage a sense of pride in female identity [Doc. 2, p. 117]. Instead of rejecting separate spheres ideology, they turned its notion of female moral superiority into a justification for women's suffrage. If the family benefited from women's purity, then bringing women into the public sphere should elevate the moral tone of public life too. This sense of female moral superiority linked the suffrage movement to other female reform movements explicitly concerned with sexuality, such as the late-nineteenth-century purity campaign (Caine, 1992).

Female suffragists used a variety of arguments for reform. Partly because the 1867 Reform Act had reinforced the connection between property ownership and enfranchisement, reformers stressed that women were the only group of tax-paying property owners denied the right to vote for their representatives [Doc. 3, p. 118]. This effectively cut through the smokescreen of antisuffrage arguments to the crucial point: suffrage was a gender issue which was resisted because it would grant women the power to undermine existing gender structures that disadvantaged them. Given the undeniable fact that the franchise was based on a property qualification, and that some women met the property requirement, suffrage opponents resorted to claims that voting was unfeminine and inconsistent with a woman's nature (Rover, 1967).

Although gender-based disabilities, such as exclusion from the franchise, encouraged women to view each other as members of a sex-class, they were divided by party affiliation, social class, religion, and political outlook. From the beginning conservatives and radicals found it difficult to work with each other. In the 1860s Emily Davies had been reluctant to help launch a public campaign for women's suffrage for fear it would attract 'wild people' [women] who 'would insist on jumping like kangaroos . . .' (Caine, 1992: 84). Davies and Frances Power Cobbe, both Conservatives, became members of the London Society's Executive Committee in the 1860s, but soon resigned because they disliked the committee's radical women.

Suffragists were also divided over men's role in the suffrage movement. When the Provisional Committee that became the London Society was being formed, Helen Taylor opposed allowing men to join. Barbara Bodichon, supported by Clementia Taylor, objected that this would delay obtaining the vote since men's cooperation would be necessary for reform. Men were included on the committee, but Helen Taylor continued to press the issue and men were excluded from the London Society's 'managing committee' (executive) when it replaced the Provisional Committee the following year (Herstein, 1985). Elsewhere men were usually welcomed; suffragists considered their participation in mixed organizations an improvement over the early Victorian practice of relegating women to female auxiliaries in reform organizations.

INTERNAL DIVISIONS

In 1871 the suffrage movement underwent the first of three major splits (the others followed in 1888 and 1915). The 1871 division arose over the relationship between the suffrage organization and the campaign to repeal the Contagious Diseases Acts directed by the Ladies' National Association for the Repeal of the Contagious Diseases Acts (LNA). Although suffragists generally opposed the Acts, many shared **Millicent Fawcett's** fear that public support for repealing the Acts would discredit the suffrage movement and therefore refused to be associated with the repeal campaign. But seventeen prominent suffragists, including the founders of suffrage societies in Edinburgh, Bristol, and Manchester considered repeal so important to women that they joined the LNA executive (Walkowitz, 1980).

In the midst of this dispute the Manchester Society initiated a change in the National Society that increased the power of the provincial societies relative to the London Society. Late in 1871 a Central Committee was established, chaired by Jacob Bright, the Manchester Society's leader. The London Society opposed this change, and refused to join the new Central Committee. The London Society itself then divided; those who believed the organized suffrage movement should not support the contagious diseases (CD) repeal campaign, such as Millicent Fawcett, retained control. The London Society then withdrew from the National Society until 1877. In addition to revealing the strong differences of opinion between radical and conservative suffragists, the split weakened the pressure for women's suffrage bills during the early 1870s when Parliament gave serious consideration to reform (Holton, 1996).

Suffragists were also divided from the beginning by the problem of how to formulate their demand. The critical issue was whether to include married women. Under the legal doctrine of coverture a married woman had no separate legal identity from her husband, and thus could not own real property. Since property ownership was required for the right to vote, proposing that women be granted the vote on the same terms as men would exclude married women.

Influenced by Conservative women such as Emily Davies and Frances Power Cobbe, the London Society initially proposed that the vote be given only to women who had 'femme sole' status – unmarried women and widows. The Manchester Society, however, reflecting the more radical views

Fawcett, Millicent Garrett (1847–1929): Fawcett became a member of the London Society for Women's Suffrage's executive when it was formed in 1867 and was the leader of the NUWSS from its formation in 1897. Although reluctant to publicly criticize WSPU militant methods, she insisted the NUWSS rely on constitutional methods and privately believed WSPU militancy after 1910 was undermining the NUWSS's efforts to win converts to the suffrage cause.

of the Bright circle, urged that married women be included in the demand. A compromise was eventually agreed upon which demanded the vote for women on the same terms as men. Since men's right to vote was based on the property qualification, this in effect excluded married women, but as it did not explicitly do so they could be included later if the property qualification was removed.

LEGISLATION PROPOSED

After John Stuart Mill was defeated in the 1868 election, Jacob Bright became the movement's parliamentary leader and introduced the first women's suffrage bill in 1870. It proposed that women be given the vote on the same terms as men, thus embodying the compromise formula which reflected the principle of sex equality. It passed its second reading with a 33 vote majority, but was defeated in the committee stage when the Prime Minister, William Gladstone, made it an issue of party loyalty by declaring his opposition. The extent of parliamentary support was significant since it would be 1897 before another suffrage bill passed its second reading. As Rendall has noted, this undermines the perception that support for women's suffrage was limited in its early years, but grew steadily in the following decades (Rendall in Vickery, 2001).

Although suffrage bills were introduced almost every year during the 1870s, the best opportunity for reform came when the Liberal Government's 1884 Reform Bill was under consideration. In order to make it acceptable to as many MPs as possible, the women's suffrage amendment to the bill was narrowly drawn; it would have enfranchised only about 100,000 women, most of them well-to-do property owners. The amendment drew considerable Conservative support since most of the proposed women voters were expected to vote Conservative. This would have partially offset the bill's enfranchisement of male rural labourers, most of whom were Liberals. But when Gladstone announced his opposition 104 MPs who had declared themselves supporters of reform voted against it, thereby causing the amendment to be rejected by a vote of 271 to 135 (Holton, 1996).

Suffragists were demoralized by the 1884 defeat because they erroneously believed it completed the extension of the franchise to men, and thus expected Parliament's interest in franchise reform to end. Upper- and middle-class women also resented the Act's implication that masculinity was valued more highly than class position. Élite women felt that enfranchising agricultural labourers, while denying the vote to the lady of the manor, undermined the social hierarchy at their expense (Rover, 1967). Frances Power Cobbe was incensed that 'a rabble of illiterates' should have been enfranchised while educated women, their social superiors, were denied the vote (Levine, 1987).

The fate of the 1884 suffrage amendment suggests why the Victorian reform movement was unsuccessful. The majority of the MPs supporting women's suffrage were Liberals, but their party loyalty was greater than their commitment to women's suffrage. Liberal Party leaders opposed reform, in part because they believed the majority of women enfranchised would vote Conservative. While Conservative Party conferences repeatedly endorsed women's suffrage, and Conservative leaders expressed support for it, they made no attempt to introduce legislation when in office, perhaps because the vast majority of Conservative MPs opposed it. This stalemate might have been overcome if public opinion had been aroused in support of reform, but Becker and other leaders preferred secret negotiations with parliamentary cliques. By the 1880s Radical suffragists in the north of England were becoming frustrated with this strategy, and urged that mass suffrage demonstrations be organized to demonstrate public support for reform (Holton, 1996).

PARTY LOYALTY

The struggle over the 1884 women's suffrage amendment increased the tendency for suffragists to polarize along party lines. Radical suffragists were incensed at Becker's willingness to support legislation enfranchising only unmarried women. Becker's tactical alliance with the Conservative Party widened the breach between herself and Liberal suffragists who advocated working through the Liberal Party. Some suffragists feared a permanent separation between reformers like Becker, who advocated allying with Conservatives for a restricted measure excluding married women, and those who insisted on working through the Liberal Party for a broader measure which would include married women (Holton, 1996).

Suffragists were also disheartened by the emergence of organized female anti-suffragism in the late 1880s. Concerned that the Conservative Government might grant suffrage to propertied spinsters and widows in the expectation they would vote Conservative, male opponents encouraged female anti-suffragists to speak out against reform. Mary Ward drafted an 'Appeal Against the Extension of the Parliamentary Franchise to Women' which was published in the *Nineteenth Century* in 1889 [**Doc. 4, p. 118**]. Reform was opposed on the ground that women's participation in politics was made impossible 'either by the disabilities of sex, or by strong formations of custom and habit resting ultimately upon physical difference . . .' (Harrison, 1978). Beatrice Potter (later Webb), Mrs Leslie Stephen, and Mrs H. H. Asquith were among the 104 prominent women who signed the

Appeal. Suffragists pointed out that many of those who signed were titled ladies whose class position ensured that they suffered less from gender disabilities than women lower in the social hierarchy [**Doc. 5, p. 119**].

The 1883 Corrupt Practices Act unintentionally increased women's participation in electoral politics substantially. By making it illegal to employ paid agents to do canvassing and other election work, the Act resulted in parties relying upon unpaid volunteers, chiefly women. Once their dependence on female volunteer workers became clear, political parties established female auxiliary organizations. The Women's Liberal Association was formed in 1887 from 63 local women's associations; by 1895 it had expanded to 448 branches with 82,000 members. The Conservative Party's Primrose League allowed women to become members shortly after it was established in 1883, and by 1891 its female membership was estimated at 500,000 (Hollis, 1987).

Party work strengthened women's conviction that they should be enfranchised, but the parties preferred that the women's organizations sub-ordinate suffrage reform to party objectives. Although the 1887 Conservative Party annual conference endorsed women's suffrage and reaffirmed support at later conferences, the Primrose League was not permitted to become a women's suffrage lobby. When the NSWS asked the League in 1886 what its position was on women's suffrage, the latter replied that the 'Executive Committee of the Ladies Grand Council cannot enter into questions of contentious politics' (Levine, 1987: 23).

Liberal women had greater autonomy. Many had been active in the suffrage movement before helping to establish Women's Liberal Associations, and intended to use the Liberal Party's women's groups to pressure the party to support women's suffrage legislation. In 1892 Gladstone's opposition to women's suffrage forced Liberal women to decide whether their highest loyalty was to the party or to suffrage reform. When pro-suffrage women gained control of the **Women's Liberal Federation** (WLF) in 1892, over 7,000 members split away to form the Women's National Liberal Association. The suffragists who remained in the WLF continued to be torn between party and gender loyalty. At the 1896 WLF annual council those giving priority to the latter proposed that members should work only for Liberal candidates who supported women's suffrage. This motion was defeated; it was replaced by one which left local women's Liberal associations free to decide (Rubinstein, 1986).

The growth of women's party organizations contributed to the 1888 NSWS split. Because it was non-party the NSWS had not allowed women's party organizations to affiliate to it. But in 1888, when several local Women's Liberal Associations requested affiliation, a majority of NSWS members voted to change the rules. Following the vote Millicent Garrett Fawcett, Lydia Becker, and their followers withdrew from the NSWS and established a rival

Women's Liberal Federation: Established in 1887. Although Catherine (Mrs William) Gladstone became its first president, Eva McClaren was its national organizer and the real moving spirit within the organization. Although some of its founders were the wives of Liberal MPs who thought the main function of the WLF should be to help their husbands gain election, the majority of WLF members believed it should help elect Liberals who supported women's causes, such as suffrage and temperance.

organization which retained the name 'Central Committee of the National Society for Women's Suffrage'. The majority of the societies adopted the new rules and formed the Central National Society for Women's Suffrage.

Fawcett, who had recently withdrawn from the Liberal Party in protest against Gladstone's Irish Home Rule policy, viewed the rules change as an attempt by Liberal Party women to take over the NSWS. The new rules did result in the affiliation of Liberal women's groups to the NSWS, thereby strengthening the influence of Liberal women within it. In addition to this controversy, the nature of the NSWS's demand was also an issue. The Central Committee continued to press for legislation which would have excluded married women. The Central National Society for Women's Suffrage was divided on the point; to avoid splitting its membership it supported bills that excluded married women as well as those which included them.

The conflict over whether married women should be included in the demand gave rise to a new suffrage society explicitly committed to that proposal: the Women's Franchise League. Begun by Elizabeth Wolstenholme Elmy in 1889, it became the voice of ultra-Radical suffragism. While the older suffrage societies were willing to drop married women from their proposed suffrage legislation in order to increase its chances of being accepted, the League rejected this compromise strategy.

The League also made special efforts to link with working-class women and with the Labour movement. The League's leaders based their claim for women's suffrage on an economic view of citizenship which implied that capitalism was part of the problem. They held that women's labor, whether it be unpaid reproductive work or paid labor, entitled them to full citizenship rights. This provided a counter to the anti-suffrage argument that the vote should be limited to men because they could be called upon to risk their lives to defend the empire (Holton, 1996).

THE 1890s REVIVAL

The 1890s have traditionally been portrayed as a decade during which the suffrage movement declined. Historians from both the constitutional and the militant movements shared this perception. Ray Strachey maintained that in 1900 the likelihood of reform seemed to be 'farther away than ever before in the history of the agitation' (Strachey, 1928). Sylvia Pankhurst described the movement as having become almost moribund in the 1890s (S. Pankhurst, 1931). This view is supported by Harrison's study of women's organizations' annual income, which indicates a sharp decline in financial support following the 1884 Reform Bill; it dropped to a low in the 1890s before reviving after 1900 (Harrison, 1983).

However, historians now view the 1890s as a reawakening of the late Victorian suffrage movement. David Rubinstein portrays the 1890s as a period of 'steady progress', and rejects the view that there was a sharp break between that decade and the following one. He cites the growth of mass support as indicated by the success of the Special Appeal in obtaining women's signatures, the widening of the movement's social base through the increased involvement of working-class women, and the origins of more militant methods as the failure of parliamentary lobbying became evident (Rubinstein, 1986). In *Suffrage Days* Sandra Holton develops this approach even further, finding the roots of militancy and democratic suffragism in new groups that were active in the 1890s, such as the Women's Franchise League (Holton, 1996). Martin Pugh concludes that these developments had created a suffragist parliamentary majority by the end of the 1890s. The parliamentary problem after 1900 was how to transform this support for the principle of women's suffrage into a specific bill that a government would allow to pass (Pugh, 2000).

Most suffrage activists were Liberals and believed that working within the Liberal Party would bring reform. They realized that the women's Liberal associations' rapid growth and the male politicians' increasing dependence on women for election work gave them leverage on the party if they chose to use it. The Scottish Women's Liberal Federation included women's suffrage among its objectives in 1891, and – warning that women were being 'turned into party machines without rights . . . to canvass for the men our party has chosen . . .' – the WLF followed suit in 1892 (Walker in Rendell, 1984: 187).

Liberal suffrage activists believed that the Liberal parliamentary party could be forced to endorse women's enfranchisement if Liberal women refused to do party work for Liberal candidates who opposed women's suffrage. This was referred to as the 'test' question. When the 1896 WLF annual council meeting rejected it in favor of allowing local associations to decide, those urging that the test question be required formed a ginger-group called the Union of Practical Suffragists (UPS) to persuade the WLF to change its position. Anticipating the WSPU's use of the test question in the 1900s, the UPS continued to press the WLF on this matter until the latter adopted the test question in 1902 (although it generated so much controversy the WLF later reversed itself) (Walker in Rendell, 1984). Although the Liberal women's pressure was not the sole factor involved, the National Liberal Federation's general committee endorsed women's suffrage in 1897, and a majority of the Liberal MPs elected in 1906 supported it.

The suffrage campaign developed greater mass support during the 1890s than in previous decades. Although the House of Commons voted against the 1892 women's suffrage bill, the bill's proponents were encouraged by the increased support (it was defeated by only 23 votes). Convinced that they could convert more MPs if they could demonstrate grass-roots support for reform, the suffrage societies organized a Special Appeal designed to refute the anti-suffragist claim that ordinary women did not care about the vote. They drafted 'An Appeal from Women of All Parties and All Classes', and for the first time made special efforts to circulate it among working-class women. By 1894 over 248,000 women had signed the Appeal, making it the largest parliamentary petition since the Chartist movement (Liddington and Norris, 1978).

Although the suffrage campaign had been mainly a middle-class movement before the 1890s, working-class women's involvement grew significantly during that decade. When the Special Appeal was launched, the Women's Co-operative Guild (WCG) encouraged its members to participate, and even though it was not circulated to some of the branches nearly one-fourth of the Guildswomen signed it (Scott, 1998). Within the WCG, the vote was portrayed as a practical step towards women's emancipation from traditional gender roles. During the discussion of the 1897 suffrage bill, Margaret Llewelyn Davies, the WCG's general secretary, warned: 'We are tired of . . . hearing that "the hand that rocks the cradle rules the world" – when a moment afterwards our brains are compared with rabbits, and we are told . . . that wives "should stay at home to wash their husbands' moleskin trousers" ' (Scott, 1998: 78).

Roper, Esther (1868–1938): Roper was secretary of the Manchester National Society for Women's Suffrage (later the North of England Society for Women's Suffrage) from 1893 to 1905. She was responsible for recruiting working-class women into the suffrage movement at a time when its members were mainly middle- and upper-class women.

By 1890 the Manchester Society for Women's Suffrage was almost moribund, but **Esther Roper**, who became its secretary in 1893, revitalized it by recruiting working-class women into the movement. The Special Appeal had acknowledged working women's concerns by noting that the lack of suffrage placed the power to restrict women's work in the hands of men who often viewed the women working alongside them as 'rivals rather than fellow workers' (Crawford, 1999: 648). Roper initiated a campaign to secure signatures from northern female textile workers to the Special Appeal that drew large numbers of working-class women into the Manchester Society. Instead of holding meetings in sedate middle-class drawing rooms, she introduced open-air meetings, often near factory gates during dinner breaks. Roper often spoke about women's suffrage at WCG and Independent Labour Party (ILP) meetings in the Manchester area, and thus also contributed to the significant increase in support within the Labour and socialist movements during the 1890s (Liddington and Norris, 1978).

The formation of the ILP in 1893 also contributed to the growth of working-class women's support for suffrage reform, especially in Scotland and the north of England. The ILP, unlike the two major parties, accepted women on an equal basis instead of shunting them into auxiliary organizations. In 1895 it officially endorsed extending electoral rights to both men and women. It also encouraged ILP women to run for local offices. Several prominent Radical Liberal suffragists, including Emmeline Pankhurst, were drawn to the ILP in part because it endorsed equality for women.

Some historians, however, have suggested that ILP men were more committed to the theory of gender equality than to its practice (Hannam and Hunt, 2001). Prior to 1895 ILP men had envisioned women as 'workers' and thus accepted them as roughly equals. But as the ILP sought a closer alliance with the trade unions after 1895, ILP men began to reflect the view of male trade unionists that waged work was unsuitable for women, and that their proper place was in the home (Ugolini in Eustance, 2000). This was accompanied by a sharply diminished interest in women's suffrage until the mid-1900s. Although some individuals like Isabella Ford remained strong voices for suffrage within the ILP, and in some regions, especially Yorkshire, suffrage support remained strong, with the exception of Keir Hardie they received little encouragement from male ILP leaders. It is unlikely that Hannah Mitchell was the only ILP woman who felt disillusioned when she discovered that many of the young ILP men who talked boldly about women's rights still expected her to make 'Sunday dinners and huge teas with home-made cakes . . . exactly like their reactionary fellows' (Mitchell, 1977: 96).

The considerable expansion in the numbers of women voting and gaining office in local elections also strengthened the parliamentary suffrage campaign during the 1890s. Although female candidates for local offices were a novelty before 1890, the number of women elected to School Boards increased from 100 to 270 during the 1890s while those elected to Poor Law Boards rose even more rapidly, from 80 to 1,147 (Pugh, 2000).

The 1894 Local Government Act made part of this increase possible, and is now viewed as a turning-point in the suffrage campaign. It was significant in that it removed the issue of coverture from the franchise reform debate by making married women eligible to vote in all the local elections in which single women and widows could. By 1900 women comprised 13.7 per cent of the local government electorate (Rubinstein, 1986). Also, by eliminating one of the important issues dividing reformers, it made the reunion of the leading suffrage organizations possible in 1897.

NUWSS FORMED

The reunion of the suffrage movement emerged out of the cooperation between the two national suffrage societies in securing some 257,000 signatures to a women's suffrage petition in the mid-1890s. Fawcett presided at the 1896 joint meeting of suffrage societies which agreed to form the National Union of Women's Suffrage Societies (NUWSS). The new organization that came into being the following year was a federation of 17 of the largest suffrage societies. Although its executive was expected to co-ordinate the member societies' activities, it had almost no power over them, and no funds of its own. During its early years the NUWSS was primarily a liaison committee linking Parliament and the member societies; it bore little resemblance to the powerful body it became later (Hume, 1982).

Fawcett's views shaped the new organization's rules. Its sole purpose was to secure votes for women, and the member societies were to be strictly neutral regarding political parties. This was a defeat for those who wanted the NUWSS to seek other gender reforms in addition to suffrage or who wanted formal ties with the Liberal Party. The Women's Franchise League, for example, did not join the NUWSS because its objectives were not limited to the vote. The NUWSS's objective was to obtain the parliamentary suffrage for women on the same terms 'as it is, or may be granted to men'.

The 1890s campaign culminated with a parliamentary majority voting for the 1897 women's suffrage bill. Introduced by a Conservative MP, Faithful Begg, following the presentation to Parliament of the signatures obtained by the Special Appeal, the bill passed its second reading with a 71 vote majority (230 to 159). This was a turning-point in parliamentary support in that it was the first of a series of parliamentary divisions in favor of women's suffrage (Pugh, 2000). Although some suffragists saw it as a sign of progress, others were frustrated because the bill did not become law even though the majority of MPs voted for it (due to the Conservative Government's refusal to allocate further time to the bill).

Suffrage activists drew different lessons from the vote. Lady Frances Balfour, president of the Central Committee of the National Society for Women's Suffrage in 1896, who was present in the House of Commons with a group of suffragists when the results of the second reading were announced, recalled a woman whispering 'incredible' in her ear, shaking hands and being kissed by a dozen others, while two other women were sobbing (Leneman, 1991). Constitutional suffragists like these considered the vote as evidence that they were winning, and that reform would come if they continued to use their current methods. But since gaining a parliamentary majority had not led to suffrage legislation others saw it as proof that the use of moderate methods had failed. This encouraged some to explore militant methods in an attempt to force the government to enact women's suffrage.

3

The Constitutional Societies, 1897–1910

The women's suffrage movement has been portrayed as being nearly moribund during the early years of the twentieth century until the Women's Social and Political Union revived it. This view assumes that the WSPU was primarily responsible for obtaining women's suffrage and underestimates the NUWSS's importance. The NUWSS was a much stronger organization by 1910 than it had been in 1900, and this improvement began around 1902, before the WSPU was founded. NUWSS income and membership rose steadily after 1902, while the number of affiliated societies increased from 17 to 31 between 1902 and 1906 (Harrison, 1983; Holton, 1986).

Although the more flamboyant WSPU overshadowed it, the NUWSS's transformation was one of the most significant developments in the suffrage movement between 1897 and 1910. At the beginning of the twentieth century the NUWSS's societies were independent bodies that carried out most of the important suffrage work. The NUWSS coordinated their activities and served as a liaison between them and Parliament, but it had little authority over them and no funds of its own. The local societies appointed the NUWSS Executive Committee members and viewed them as their representatives (Hume, 1982).

The NUWSS initiated a more aggressive stage in the suffrage campaign by convening a National Convention in Defence of the Civic Rights of Women in 1903. With a general election approaching, the delegates requested the NUWSS to immediately form a committee in every electoral district to press the question of women's suffrage on every parliamentary candidate before the election, and to attempt to persuade local party associations to select only candidates committed to women's suffrage. In order to implement this scheme the NUWSS began to exercise greater control over its member societies and shifted its focus from Parliament to the parliamentary constituencies. All of the candidates in the 1906 general election were questioned about their position on women's suffrage, and 415 pledged support for it (Hume, 1982). In this and in subsequent elections prior to 1912 the

NUWSS election policy was straightforward: identify the candidate who was the best friend of women's suffrage and canvass the constituency on his behalf. Officially it was a non-party policy, but because Liberals dominated the NUWSS it usually resulted in the Liberal candidate being endorsed (Hirshfield, 1990).

The Women's Liberal Federation also intervened in the election to pressure Liberal candidates to support suffrage. Liberal suffragists had long maintained that Liberal women were being used as 'Political Charwomen' – that is, they did the candidates' electoral dirty work even though the party did not consider them suitable voters. At its 1902 annual Council meeting the WLF adopted a resolution forbidding its executive from assisting anti-suffrage candidates. The WLF's national office ordinarily provided experienced female activists to conduct canvassing in the local constituencies; this was especially important during by-elections. Although local associations were exempt from the ban, the denial of the national office's trained operatives could substantially diminish a candidate's prospects. In thirteen of the twenty by-elections between May 1904 and November 1905 the Liberal candidate pledged in writing to vote for women's suffrage; assistance was denied in five of the seven by-elections in which the candidate refused to pledge (Hirshfield, 1990).

THE NEW LIBERAL GOVERNMENT

There was a surge of optimism within the NUWSS when the 1906 Liberal Government was formed and the majority of MPs were pledged to women's suffrage. Although officially non-party, the NUWSS considered women's suffrage a natural extension of liberal principles and had always assumed the Liberal Party would enfranchise women. Underlying this conviction was the mistaken belief that reform would emerge when a majority of backbenchers had been intellectually converted to the justice of the cause. Even though most Liberals supported women's suffrage, party and electoral considerations blocked reform: the party was so deeply divided that proceeding with reform risked a party split, while granting the NUWSS demand for equal suffrage rights was expected to enfranchise women who would be mainly Conservative voters.

The NUWSS's confidence in the Liberal Government was jolted almost immediately. The Prime Minister, Henry Campbell-Bannerman, met with a deputation from it and other women's societies, but refused to make any pledge regarding suffrage and bluntly informed them that the government was not likely to introduce legislation. Margaret Ashton, the Women's Liberal Federation's spokeswoman, was so disillusioned by Campbell-Bannerman's reply that she began working for Labour Party candidates. This became increasingly common in the following years (Vellacott, 1993).

THE MUD MARCH

WSPU militancy in 1906 generated considerable publicity which increased women's support for suffrage, and left the NUWSS seeking new ways to prove that it was equally vigorous in fighting for reform [**Doc. 6, p. 120**]. It responded by organizing a series of open-air processions to demonstrate mass support for reform. The first of these, the February 1907 'Mud March', was the largest open-air demonstration ever held at that point. Although some 3,000 women representing forty organizations participated, the WSPU did not, because the Women's Liberal Federation refused to take part if the WSPU was invited (Tickner, 1988). The Mud March had a considerable impact because of the novelty of the spectacle, but even more so because of the impropriety of respectable women marching in the streets. Participating required a degree of courage beyond that needed for subsequent processions; the marchers risked their reputations, their employment, and ridicule from the crowds.

Prior to 1907 the NUWSS's decentralization of authority hampered effective action, but the new constitution adopted that year substantially strengthened the national organization, including its executive committee. Previously the executive committee members had viewed themselves as delegates representing the constituent societies which appointed them. But the new constitution provided for a longer term in that position, thus encouraging them to view issues from the NUWSS's perspective. Under the new constitution the executive committee was responsible to a Council of representatives from the local societies that met quarterly to set policies. Following the new constitution's adoption, the NUWSS for the first time moved into its own offices, hired full-time staff, and controlled its own funds (Hume, 1982). Although the reorganization was intended to make the NUWSS a more effective fighting force, it also drew attention to the contrast between its democratic governing structure and the WSPU's.

The new constitution also strengthened Millicent Fawcett's authority to speak for the NUWSS by providing for an elected President. Fawcett did not assume this position uncontested. Delegates at the 1907 Council meeting elected her over Lady Frances Balfour, President of the London Society for Women's Suffrage (LSWS) and sister-in-law of Arthur Balfour, the Conservative Party leader (Rubinstein, 1991).

If the NUWSS's faith in the Liberal Party as a vehicle of reform seems excessive, it was not due to Fawcett's personal loyalty to that party. She left the Liberal Party in protest against Gladstone's Irish Home Rule Bill and never returned. Fawcett became a Liberal Unionist, but in 1904 resigned from the Women's Liberal Unionist Association when it supported the Conservative Party's policy of protection. Although her commitment to free trade prevented her from belonging to the Conservative and Unionist Party, her biographer defines her political position as 'Unionist-leaning' (Rubinstein, 1991: 183). As late as 1910 she publicly attacked key Liberal Government policies, and remained resolutely hostile to Irish Home Rule even though it was a central part of the Liberal Government's legislative programme after 1910.

Conservative women's importance in the NUWSS, and in the suffrage movement in general, has been underestimated. Fawcett considered Lady Balfour to be her first lieutenant; Balfour was one of the NUWSS's founders and had been a dominant figure in the LSWS for many years. Conservative members of the Strachey family became increasingly important in both the NUWSS and the LSWS in the decade prior to the First World War. Lady Jane Strachey was one of the three women (along with Fawcett and Lady Balfour) who led the 1907 Mud March, and later became a member of the NUWSS's Executive. Her daughter, Pippa, was elected to the LSWS Executive in 1906 and served as its secretary from 1907 until 1951. Pippa's sister-in-law, Ray, became the LSWS's Chair in 1913 and the NUWSS's parliamentary secretary in 1915 (Caine, 2005).

Conservative and Unionist Women's Franchise Association: Established in 1907 with Lady Selborne as president. Comprising Conservative Party women, it attempted to convert Conservatives to the suffrage cause.

Lady Selborne, the daughter of former Prime Minister Lord Salisbury, and Arthur Balfour's cousin, became President of the **Conservative and Unionist Women's Franchise Association** (CUWFA) when it was formed in 1907. The CUWFA lobbied the Conservative Party for women's suffrage. Although they considered encouraging Conservative women to refuse to do election work for anti-suffrage Conservative candidates, they concentrated on convincing Conservatives that granting the vote to women who met existing property qualifications had important electoral advantages for the party. The CUWFA claimed that in addition to enfranchising women who would mainly be Conservative voters, a limited measure of women's suffrage was the best means of heading off the movement for adult male suffrage (Morgan, 1975). By 1913 the CUWFA had 53 branches, more than its better-publicized Liberal counterpart.

INTERNAL TENSIONS

The NUWSS included suffragists from across the political spectrum, and unsurprisingly there were sharp clashes reflecting divergent class and political outlook. The split between democratic suffragists, mainly from the northern societies, and Conservative suffragists, who dominated the LSWS, was a growing source of tension within the NUWSS after 1907. The 1907 constitution granted the NUWSS executive greater power over policy-making at the expense of the provincial societies, and the latter were dissatis-fied with the continued control of the executive by Conservative women, many of whom were LSWS members. The struggle culminated at the 1910 council meeting which, over the objections of the executive and the LSWS, adopted a more decentralized structure including the formation of regional federations (Vellacott, 1993).

Historians traditionally have portrayed the NUWSS and the WSPU as rivals, and stressed the differences between them. Sandra Holton, however, suggests that, at least until 1909, they should be viewed as two wings of the same movement in a 'symbiotic' relationship (Holton, 1986). Jo Vellacott agrees, although she views the break between the two organizations as occur-ring around 1908 when the WSPU shifted to window-breaking in addition to disrupting Liberal meetings (Vellacott, 1993). Both agree that tensions between the groups increased substantially after 1909; by 1914 Fawcett con-sidered the WSPU militants to be the 'chief obstacles' to achieving suffrage (Rubinstein, 1991: 177).

Although some NUWSS members had reservations about the WSPU, these tended to be suppressed until 1908 because the militants were strengthening the suffrage movement. NUWSS members often sympathized with the early forms of militancy which involved civil disobedience without harming property or other persons. In 1906 Fawcett admitted that in the past twelve months militancy had done more to make suffrage 'practical politics' than constitutional methods had in the past 12 years, and acknowledged that the WSPU's activities had contributed significantly to the NUWSS's membership growth after 1905 (Rubinstein, 1991). Until 1908 many WSPU members also belonged to the NUWSS, and both organizations accepted this without any sense of inconsistency (Holton, 1986).

The NUWSS support for militancy was strongest when it involved women becoming martyrs for the suffrage cause by undergoing arrest and imprison-ment. But NUWSS opinion swung against the WSPU when it changed in 1908 to attacks on property and people. Reluctant to criticize it publicly, Fawcett privately thought the WSPU's encouraging working-class 'toughs' and unemployed workers to join them in using 'brute force' to rush the House of Commons in 1908 was the act of a 'dastard' or a woman gone 'mad' **[Doc. 7, p. 121]** (Hume, 1982). In November 1908 the NUWSS made the breach public by sending a letter to MPs and the press expressing its 'strong objection' to the use of violence, and officially dissociating itself from the WSPU (Rubinstein, 1991). Shortly afterwards, it declined a WSPU invitation to join in a united demonstration, stating that there were 'questions of principle at stake' which made it essential that the constitutional suffragists 'separate themselves completely from those who employ different methods' (Tickner, 1988: 111).

The conflict between the NUWSS and the WSPU centered on the merits of militant methods, but it also raised ideological differences. Fawcett's belief that women's nature was different and morally superior to men's underlay her objection to the WSPU's resort to force [Doc. 8, p. 121]. Given her conviction that the women's suffrage movement was 'an appeal against government by physical force', it is not surprising that she viewed the WSPU's use of force as undermining the movement's moral foundation. By resorting to force and behaving like men, the WSPU not only undermined the ideology of sexual difference, it also undermined the notion of female moral superiority, thus, in Fawcett's view, weakening women's claim for the franchise (Holton in Smith, 1990).

Although Fawcett's efforts to prevent conflict between the NUWSS and the WSPU had allowed suffrage advocates to belong to both organizations, by 1908 the NUWSS had become so alarmed at the WSPU's tactics that it officially committed its members to using only 'constitutional' methods. This placed pressure on WSPU members who also belonged to NUWSS local societies to choose between the two; open conflict developed in some societies. Constitutionalists and WSPU supporters struggled for control of the London Society for Women's Suffrage in 1908 following the NUWSS's public condemnation of militant methods. At the 1908 LSWS annual meeting four WSPU members who also belonged to the LSWS formally proposed that the LSWS adopt the WSPU's anti-Liberal by-election policy, and that LSWS executive committee members not be allowed to hold office in party organizations, a move intended to exclude Liberal women from the LSWS executive (Hume, 1982).

The NUWSS and LSWS executives viewed this as a WSPU attempt to seize control of the LSWS, and in a tense struggle succeeded in defeating both resolutions. Fawcett spoke against the resolutions, urging LSWS members to resign if they could not accept the NUWSS policy of opposition to unlawful methods. During the following three months 133 LSWS members did resign, but 293 new members joined (Holton, 1986).

Women's Freedom League: Established in 1907 by WSPU members who opposed the Pankhursts' split with the Labour movement. Charlotte Despard became its president. Its journal, *The Vote*, was issued from 1909 to 1933.

The NUWSS began publishing its own journal as a result of the clash with the WSPU. Previously it contributed to *The Women's Franchise*, an independent suffrage journal which also printed reports from the WSPU and the **Women's Freedom League** (WFL). Not wanting the public to link them with the militant groups, the NUWSS established *The Common Cause* in 1909. Edited originally by Helena Swanwick, by 1912 it had a circulation of 10,000 (Rubinstein, 1991).

The journal's title drew attention to a distinction between the NUWSS and the WSPU which grew in importance after 1910. While the latter viewed itself as a women's movement promoting gender solidarity, the NUWSS accepted male members, rejected 'setting the women against men', and considered itself to be working for the 'common cause of humanity' (Holton, 1986: 66). Fawcett recognized that allowing anti-suffragists to portray the suffrage campaign as part of a sex-war waged by women would hamper efforts to persuade an all-male Parliament to pass suffrage legislation, but she also sincerely believed that a sex-war was impossible [**Doc. 9, p. 121**].

In other respects, however, the NUWSS and the WSPU's ideologies were similar. Both drew upon a heightened gender consciousness which encouraged an unusual degree of gender unity between women of different classes. Although the WSPU's concern with women's sexual exploitation is better known, Barbara Caine has drawn attention to its importance in Fawcett's ideology (Caine, 1992). Some NUWSS members, such as Lady Chance, viewed the women's movement as a great moral movement, and claimed that the suffrage demand was rooted in the belief that women would not be able to eradicate the evils arising from male sexual exploitation of women until they had the vote [**Doc. 10, p. 122**] (Kent, 1987).

Anti-suffragists used the women's rhetoric of gender unity to claim that masculinity was under attack, and to urge that men bond together to resist this subversive movement. The suffrage campaign's gender dimensions thus created special problems for its male supporters (John and Eustance, 1997). Anti-suffragists impugned their masculinity and denounced them as 'traitors to the masculine cause'. Despite this, male suffrage organizations sprang up in various parts of Britain: the Men's League for Women's Suffrage (established 1907) was based in London; the Manchester Men's League for Women's Suffrage was created in 1908; and Scottish men formed the Northern Men's Federation for Women's Suffrage in 1913. The men's organizations undermined the anti-suffragist claim that the suffrage struggle was part of a sex-war in which masculinity implied opposition to women's suffrage.

Early in 1908 a Liberal MP, Henry Stanger, introduced a Private Member's bill on women's suffrage. The NUWSS felt very encouraged when it passed its Second Reading with a 179 vote majority, even though it was not granted parliamentary time to proceed further. This was the first occasion since 1897 that Parliament had acted favorably on a women's suffrage bill, and the bill's substantial Liberal support strengthened the NUWSS conviction that the Liberal Party would enact reform (Hume, 1982).

This strategy became questionable when Henry Asquith, a determined anti-suffragist, became Prime Minister later in 1908. Shortly after he assumed office, a deputation of 60 Liberal MPs met with Asquith to request that additional parliamentary time be provided for the Stanger bill. Although he admitted that about two-thirds of the Cabinet and a majority of the Liberal Party favored reform, Asquith refused. Instead, he proposed that the government sponsor a manhood-suffrage bill which could be amended to include women's suffrage, and pledged that he would not oppose such an amendment if it were 'democratic'. NUWSS leaders viewed this as a ruse to placate the women's suffrage advocates while avoiding reform. Asquith realized that many of the MPs who supported equal franchise rights would not support a measure extending it to all women. While appearing to grant a concession, he was actually ensuring its defeat by insisting that the amendment be 'democratic'. Asquith confirmed this interpretation a few days later when he acknowledged in Parliament that he did not expect suffrage legislation in the foreseeable future (Morgan, 1975).

DEMOCRATIC SUFFRAGISTS

Asquith's support for an adult suffrage measure heightened the tensions between reformers urging women's enfranchisement as part of an adult suffrage measure and those, like Fawcett, who advocated the franchise for women on the same terms that men had it. Encouraged by Asquith's pledge, in 1909 women trade unionists joined with the Women's Co-operative Guild (WCG) and the Women's Labour League to establish the **People's Suffrage Federation** (PSF) to work for adult suffrage. Led by Margaret Llewelyn Davies, the WCG's general secretary, the PSF believed that working-class women should be included in suffrage reform, and that this could best be achieved by linking women's suffrage to the movement for a democratic franchise. Davies coined the term 'democratic suffragists' to refer to those who took this approach (Holton, 1986).

People's Suffrage Federation: Established in 1909 by women trade unionists and Women's Co-operative Guild members. Led by Margaret Llewelyn Davies, the WCG's secretary, it advocated adult suffrage in order that working-class women would gain the right to vote.

Davies and her supporters saw several advantages to pressing for adult suffrage. They believed that class divisions were undermining suffragist efforts to create a sense of gender solidarity. Democratic suffragists objected to equal franchise because granting the vote to élite propertied women would reinforce the class structure. Adult suffrage, however, would avoid this by enfranchising working-class women. It also had greater partisan appeal to Liberals than equal suffrage. Many Liberals feared that the NUWSS demand for suffrage on the same basis as men would enfranchise women likely to vote Conservative, whereas adult suffrage would increase the number of Liberal voters (Vellacott, 1993).

Both WSPU and NUWSS leaders opposed adult suffrage. Fawcett did not think there was any great pressure in the country for adult suffrage, and was convinced the change would make reform much more difficult to achieve. But there was significant support for adult suffrage within the NUWSS; its secretary, Marion Phillips, had been one of the PSF founders. Convinced that adult suffrage was a trap, Fawcett prevented democratic suffragists from changing NUWSS policy; Phillips resigned as NUWSS secretary in 1910, apparently as a result of the conflict (Rubinstein, 1991).

ORGANIZED ANTI-SUFFRAGE OPPOSITION

Anti-suffragists were so alarmed by the improved prospects for reform in 1908 that they began to organize. A parliamentary committee of male anti-suffragists urged female opponents to set up an organization to resist reform. In July 1908 the **Women's National Anti-Suffrage League** (WNAL) was established with Lady Jersey chairing the executive committee, but with Mrs Humphrey Ward as the real driving force within the organization. Later that year it merged with the men's anti-suffrage league to form the National League for Opposing Women's Suffrage. By 1914 it had 42,000 members, many of them wealthy and influential. Lord Rothschild was the anti-suffrage league's leading financial supporter, while the others included some of Britain's most prominent bankers, brewers, and coal and steel magnates (Harrison, 1978).

Women's National Anti-Suffrage League: Established in 1908. Although Lady Jersey chaired its executive committee, Mrs Humphrey Ward, the popular novelist, was the real driving force within the organization. It merged with the men's anti-suffrage league later in 1908 and became the National League for Opposing Women's Suffrage.

Female anti-suffragists presented a variety of arguments against women voting in parliamentary elections. Most of these were based on assumptions about sexual difference linked to the idea of separate spheres. Violet Markham, prominent in the WNAL, insisted that women's nature had a distinct spiritual quality that men lacked. She feared that women would lose their special qualities and sink to the men's level if they entered political life on equal terms with men. While she urged women to participate in local government because it involved areas such as education which were part of women's sphere, she did not think women were suited to vote in parliamentary elections which were concerned with the defence of the empire and thus beyond women's experience. While her objection rested in part on women's supposed lack of knowledge about an area outside their sphere, it also stemmed from a conviction that matters involving physical force were part of the male sphere. Many female anti-suffragists, including Markham, feared that participation in decisions to use physical force would corrupt women's spiritual nature and erode the differences between women and men.

Some earlier accounts portrayed the NUWSS as a group of self-interested middle-class women narrowly concerned with the vote to enhance their status. This is misleading in several respects. The NUWSS believed that the vote would transform gender relationships and women's place in society. It maintained that women would gain economic independence, more job opportunities, higher wages, and better marriages from the vote (Garner, 1984). It was the NUWSS member, Ada Nield Chew, who attacked 'the ideal of the domestic tabby cat woman as that to which all womanhood should aspire' (Garner, 1984: 20). Chew considered the assumption that all women are especially suited for domestic tasks to be as absurd as claiming all men are suited to be engineers.

SCOTLAND AND WALES

Historians have recently begun to explore the implications of national identity for the women's suffrage movement. Although the NUWSS and the WSPU portrayed themselves as British women's movements, both were led by English women who tended to view the struggle from an English perspective. While welcoming the emergence of a British women's movement, Irish, Welsh, and Scottish women were aware that it could become an instrument of English cultural hegemony.

The NUWSS had greater success than the WSPU in establishing Welsh branches, partly because it relied on Welsh women in building a democratic organization (Leneman in Joannou and Purvis, 1998). By 1913 the Cardiff and District Women's Suffrage Society was the largest NUWSS society outside of London. The NUWSS recognized that the Welsh Home Rule movement could benefit the suffrage campaign; NUWSS lobbying helped ensure that the 1914 Welsh Home Rule Bill granted women the right to vote for the proposed Welsh regional parliament (Vellacott, 1993).

In contrast to Wales, Scotland had a vigorous suffrage movement that was well-established before the twentieth century. The Edinburgh Society for Women's Suffrage was one of the original five societies that had sponsored John Stuart Mill's 1866 suffrage petition. Scottish suffrage societies secured about two million signatures to suffrage petitions between 1867 and 1876, a remarkable display of support given Scotland's relatively small population (Leneman, 1991). The Glasgow and West of Scotland Association for Women's Suffrage was established in 1902, an indication that the Scottish movement was already thriving when the WSPU emerged. Insisting on a greater degree of independence than the Welsh women's societies, the NUWSS's Scottish branches joined together in the Scottish Federation of the NUWSS in 1909; by 1914 it included 63 societies with 7,370 members (Leneman, 1991: 189).

Scottish women, campaigning under the slogan, 'ye mauna tramp on the Scottish thistle', developed a suffrage movement with a distinct Scottish identity. Although they shared a sense of gender unity with English women, Scottish women resisted the imposition of an English cultural identity on the Scottish movement. They protested when the NUWSS referred to its 1911 suffrage procession (which included Scottish women) as the 'March of England's Women' (Burton, 1994). The Scottish women also brought about the dismissal of at least one English organizer the NUWSS sent to Scotland, claiming that she was incompatible with the Scots.

It would be misleading to assume that the NUWSS's Scottish societies meekly accepted whatever policies the NUWSS's national officers attempted to impose on them. Many Scottish suffragists were also Liberal Party activists, and thus were torn by the conflict between their loyalty to suffrage reform and to a party that refused to grant it. Given that Scotland was the Liberal Party's strongest base, it is not surprising that some Scottish societies resisted the NUWSS's 1912 electoral alliance with the Labour Party. The Scottish Federation of the NUWSS precipitated a constitutional struggle within the NUWSS when it established its own Electoral Fighting Fund (EFF) committee, since the latter appeared to have been created to prevent effective EFF work in Scotland. Although a compromise resolved the issue, the conflict demonstrated how difficult it was for the NUWSS to implement its policies in regions where there was substantial local opposition (Leneman, 1991).

CHURCH AND UNIVERSITY SOCIETIES

Further research on the relationship between religion and the suffrage movement is needed. Although church membership is often assumed to have made women less likely to participate in female reform movements such as the suffrage campaign, it is clear that religion strengthened some women's commitment to reform (de Vries, 1998).

Catholic feminists established the **Catholic Women's Suffrage Society** (CWSS) early in 1911 to draw Catholic women into the suffrage campaign. Although some individual members were active in the WSPU or the WFL, the CWSS became a constitutional society with branches in Liverpool and Wimbledon; by 1913 it claimed 1,000 members. It participated in the London coronation procession in 1911, and signed the Jewish League's resolution against forced feeding of suffrage prisoners; its leaders supported the Tax Resistance League until the CWSS rank-and-file objected (Mason, 1986).

Catholic Women's Suffrage Society: Established in 1911 and open to Catholics of both sexes who supported women's parliamentary suffrage. After 1918 it became St Joan's Social and Political Alliance.

Church of England women's participation in the suffrage campaign grew out of a prior campaign for women's right to vote in church councils. Many of them joined the Church League for Women's Suffrage, formed in 1909, which was led by the Reverend Claude Hinscliff and Maude Royden. A constitutional society, it had over 5,000 members by April 1914. Some of its members established the Suffragist Churchwomen's Protest Committee; in 1914 Alice Kidd, its secretary, informed the Archbishop of Canterbury that the committee objected to the 'servile attitude of the Heads of the Church towards an unjust and irresponsible government' (Heeney, 1988: 106).

Most universities had suffrage societies prior to 1914: Cambridge, Oxford, Glasgow, Edinburgh, and St Andrews were among those with active groups. Cambridge students were among the most active. Both Girton and Newnham had established suffrage societies by 1907 (they merged in 1908 to create the Cambridge University Women's Suffrage Society). One parent (Philip Bagenal) lamented that his perfectly sensible daughter had turned into a suffragist at Newnham, and warned that Cambridge had become a 'manu-factory' of very advanced women (Tickner, 1988: 210d). Most female students who were active were associated with the NUWSS; in June 1908, for example, the Cambridge University Women's Suffrage Society provided 300 marchers for the NUWSS London procession (Crawford, 1999: 94). But the WSPU's image was so appealing that even young NUWSS members like Dorothy and Pippa Strachey – both committed to constitutional methods – referred to themselves as suffragettes (Caine, 2005: 296).

With a general election approaching, Liberal women were torn between gender and party loyalty. Asquith's opposition to women's suffrage prompted demands that Liberal women refuse to do election work for Liberal candid-ates who were not proven friends of reform, and pressure within the NUWSS to adopt an anti-Liberal election policy. The issue became a matter of heated controversy in 1909 when Caroline Osler, President of an NUWSS affiliate, the Birmingham Suffrage Society, appeared on the platform with Asquith at a Liberal Party rally shortly after a suffragist meeting to protest against the exclusion of women from Asquith's meetings. Attacked publicly for placing party loyalty ahead of the suffrage cause, Osler resigned from her position in the local WLF shortly afterwards. Three other officers in the local WLF followed her example, and *The Common Cause* reported other women's resignations from their WLF positions around this time. In 1910 the NUWSS rules were changed to require officers and executive committee members to pledge that they would 'put the interests of suffrage before party considera-tions' (Holton, 1986: 50).

The announcement of the January 1910 general election revived optimism about the prospects for reform. Responding to pressure from the Women's Liberal Federation, Asquith pledged at the beginning of the election cam-paign that the Liberal Government, if returned to office, would allow a free vote in the House of Commons on a women's suffrage amendment to a Reform Bill. Winston Churchill and Edward Grey also made encouraging statements about women's suffrage, leaving the impression that reform was likely if a majority of MPs supported it. In addition to pressuring candidates to include women's suffrage in their election addresses, the NUWSS organized voters' petitions at polling places to demonstrate that male voters supported women's suffrage. In some places hostile police warned the suffragists that if they asked voters for signatures to the petition, they might be arrested for solicitation under the law intended to deal with prostitutes. Despite impediments such as this, almost 300,000 signatures were obtained and the NUWSS viewed it as a useful demonstration of male electoral support for the cause (Vellacott, 1993). Although 323 members of the new House of Commons were pledged to some version of reform, the Liberal Party lost its majority and in the following years depended upon support from the Labour Party and the Irish Nationalists to remain in office.

The Liberal Government's precarious position created an opportunity for suffragists to exert even greater pressure when a second general election became necessary in December 1910. Although the Women's Liberal Federation's executive committee refused to endorse any action that might jeopardize a Liberal victory, the acrimony generated by the debate at the 1910 WLF annual meeting demonstrated that some Liberal women activists were no longer willing to work for the re-election of a Liberal Government not firmly committed to reform. This alarmed Liberal MPs who realized that active support by Liberal women party workers was vital to their election prospects. One Liberal MP, Walter MacLaren, warned the Liberal Chief Whip, the Master of Elibank, that the party could not afford to alienate Liberal women party workers, and therefore should pledge that it would provide facilities for a women's suffrage bill in the next parliament (Morgan, 1975). About two weeks later Asquith made such a pledge, thus permitting the NUWSS and Liberal women to work for Liberal candidates considered friends of reform.

The suffrage campaign made substantial progress during the first decade of the twentieth century. The NUWSS began its transformation from an organization dominated by middle-class London women to a national movement with a much broader social base among women from a variety of ethnic, religious, and class backgrounds. Whereas prior to 1900 suffragists were still seeking to persuade MPs of the merits of the issue, by 1910 a majority had been converted to the cause (Pugh, 2000). What remained was to determine what version of reform would be acceptable to Parliament, and to find a means of forcing the government either to sponsor legislation or at least not to impede passage of a bill favored by a parliamentary majority.

4

The Militant Societies, 1903–14

The militant women's suffrage campaign's historiography has changed dramatically. While the Women's Social and Political Union remains center stage, there is greater awareness that many militants were active in other groups: the Women's Freedom League, the Men's Political Union, the Women's Tax Resistance League, the East London Federation of Suffragettes, and the United Suffragists. Furthermore, it is increasingly clear that there is much more to the militant campaign than the Pankhurst family history; 'free-lance' activists often conducted the militant campaign outside London with considerable independence from WSPU headquarters. Historians used to believe that the militants were distinguished from the constitutional suffragists by militant actions, but since some activists belonged to both groups it is clear that at the grass-roots level – at least until 1908 – there was no rigid distinction between them (Stanley and Morley, 1988). Although the militant campaign used to be viewed as a radical break with the past, we now perceive its roots in nineteenth-century popular Radicalism, including the Radical suffragists in the Women's Franchise League (Holton, 1996). While earlier accounts portrayed militancy as a single tactic, it is the diversity in the forms of militancy that now seems significant. Although non-historians often assume the WSPU was primarily responsible for obtaining women's suffrage, historians are much more sceptical about its contribution. It is generally agreed that the WSPU revitalized the suffrage campaign initially, but that its escalation of militancy after 1912 impeded reform. Recent studies have shifted from claiming that the WSPU was responsible for women's suffrage to portraying it as an early form of radical feminism that sought to liberate women from a male-centered gender system (Purvis, 2002).

Despite the considerable body of scholarship devoted to the militant campaign, its history remains contested ground. There are two main schools of interpretation offering alternative frameworks for understanding it: the socialist-feminist and the radical-feminist. The differences between them

originated with Sylvia and **Christabel Pankhurst**'s conflicting interpretations. While Sylvia stressed the links between the militant campaign and the
socialist and labour movements, Christabel claimed that an independent
women's movement was needed because working-class men were no more
reliable as allies than men from other classes. Socialist-feminist historians
such as Sandra Holton accept much of Sylvia's approach and view the
militant campaign as part of a social movement seeking to reduce class distinctions and create a more democratic society. Radical-feminist historians
like June Purvis question the validity of many of Sylvia's claims, and suggest
the struggle resembled a sex-war more than class conflict. While both sides
agree that the militant campaign undermined traditional stereotypes of
femininity and stimulated a heightened sense of gender conflict, there is no
consensus on several key issues regarding the militant campaign (Holton in
Purvis and Holton, 2000).

Although earlier accounts often implied that the militant suffrage
movement began with the WSPU's formation in 1903, recent research has
drawn attention to its origins in the 1890s Radical suffragists' campaigns.
The Radical suffragists worked through several organizations: the **North
of England Society for Women's Suffrage** (NESWS) (affiliated with
the NUWSS; previously the Manchester National Society), the Women's
Franchise League, and the Women's Emancipation Union. They were considered radical in part because they sought complete gender equality rather
than just equal suffrage rights. At the Women's Franchise League's initial
meeting in 1889, Alice Scatcherd conveyed the League's militant spirit by
encouraging women to revolt against Victorian feminine virtues, especially
women's 'self-effacement', thus anticipating the WSPU's subsequent assault
on the 'slave-spirit' that held women in bondage (Purvis, 2002: 31). The
Radical suffragists also introduced several aspects of the militant suffrage
campaign that the WSPU is often assumed to have begun a decade later:
impatience with the NUWSS's cautious approach; disillusionment with the
Liberal Party followed by the adoption of a non-party position; recruiting
working-class women; and a more confrontational style of suffrage campaigning that included open-air meetings, passive resistance, and civil disobedience (Holton, 1996). The connections between the Radical suffragists
and the WSPU were personal as well as organizational. Emmeline Pankhurst,
one of the Women's Franchise League's founders, was a member of its
executive committee and through her friendships with the Radical suffragists
in it and other groups became acquainted with the methods that later
characterized the WSPU's campaign. Several prominent Radical suffragists
supported the WSPU after it was formed; the best known, Elizabeth
Wolstenholme Elmy, remained close to the Pankhursts and became a
member of the WSPU's (executive) committee (Holton, 1996).

Pankhurst, Christabel
(1880–1958): Emmeline
Pankhurst's eldest daugh-
ter. One of the earliest
WSPU members, she
introduced militant
methods into the WSPU
suffrage campaign. After
1907 she and her
mother emerged as the
dominant figures within
the WSPU.

**North of England Society
for Women's Suffrage:**
The new name given to
the Manchester National
Society for Women's
Suffrage when it affiliated
to the National Union of
Women's Suffrage Soci-
eties in 1897. With Esther
Roper as its secretary, it
was especially concerned
with drawing working-
class women into the
suffrage movement.

Emmeline Pankhurst had been active in the women's suffrage campaign for nearly a quarter of a century prior to founding the WSPU. She became a member of the executive committee of the Manchester National Society for Women's Suffrage in 1880; became the Women's Franchise League's joint secretary in 1890; and, in 1893, after returning to Manchester, she served again on the Manchester National Society's executive committee. After she joined the Independent Labour Party in 1894, most of her political work during the following decade involved the ILP (she was, for example, elected to the Manchester School Board as an ILP candidate in 1900). At the 1902 ILP Annual Conference she moved a successful resolution that the ILP should take immediate steps to secure suffrage for women on the same terms 'on which it is or may be granted to men' (Purvis, 2002: 58).

But it soon appeared that, apart from Keir Hardie, the male ILP leaders had little interest in women's suffrage. Most preferred adult suffrage, and left ambiguous the question of whether they meant it to include all adult women. By March 1903 Emmeline's oldest daughter, Christabel, had already begun public criticism of the newly formed Labour Representation Committee (from which the Labour Party emerged) for its indifference towards women's suffrage, and was encouraging her mother to work independently of the labour movement for that reform (Purvis, 2002).

When the Pankhursts were considering forming a new women's organization, a vigorous women's suffrage movement already existed in the north of England. Led by Esther Roper and Eva Gore-Booth, the North of England Society for Women's Suffrage concentrated on securing working-class women's support by working with local labour and trade union organizations (in 1903 many of the Radical suffragists split off to form the Lancashire and Cheshire Women Textile and Other Workers' Representation Committee to work for adult women's suffrage, rather than the equal suffrage rights the WSPU advocated). Christabel had been drawn into the NESWS in 1901, and was a member of its executive committee from 1902 until 1905. She later acknowledged serving her political apprenticeship in the suffrage movement under Roper and Gore-Booth (C. Pankhurst, 1959). But by 1903 Christabel had begun to rebel against their leadership. She considered Labour's support for women's suffrage to be half-hearted, and had little enthusiasm for the drudgery involved in building a mass organization by grass-roots political work (Liddington and Norris, 1978). It is not surprising, therefore, that she encouraged her mother to form a new women's suffrage organization that was not affiliated with either the labour movement or the NUWSS.

Mrs Pankhurst, convinced that the ILP firmly supported women's suffrage, was shocked when she discovered that several key ILP leaders were either indifferent to or actually hostile to it. Her sense of betrayal was encouraged by Christabel, who denied that the ILP was especially favorable towards gender equality, and in the ILP's own journal warned that working-class men were 'as unjust to women as men of other classes' (Purvis, 2002: 66). This new awareness that ILP support for women's suffrage could not be taken for granted contributed to Mrs Pankhurst's decision to form a women's organization to campaign for it.

Emmeline Pankhurst established the Women's Social and Political Union in October 1903 by inviting a small group of working-class women, most of them wives of ILP members, to her home in Manchester. Although the WSPU rivalled the NUWSS in importance later in the decade, it grew slowly; by the summer of 1905 it had no more than thirty members. During its early years most of its members were working-class women supplemented by a few middle-class women like the Pankhursts who were active in the labour movement. The WSPU's original speakers were working-class women, most of them ILP members: **Teresa Billington** (**Billington-Greig** after her marriage in 1907), Annie Kenney, and Hannah Mitchell. Mary Gawthorpe, who became one of the WSPU's most effective speakers, had been the Leeds ILP's vice president before joining the WSPU in 1906. Because of their ILP connection, they were accustomed to holding open-air meetings and to the politics of disruption, methods which had not been part of the London suffrage campaign until the WSPU introduced them.

Sceptical of the men's commitment, from the beginning the WSPU was a women-only group originally intended to pressure the ILP to make a firm commitment to women's suffrage. Within the labour movement the WSPU was perceived in its early years as the ILP's women's organization, even though it was not formally affiliated to it (Purvis, 2002). Although it shared the NUWSS's demand for the vote on the same terms as it was, or would be, granted to men, it differed in excluding men from membership and in its strategy. While the NUWSS attempted to create cross-party support for a private member's bill, the WSPU considered it crucial that the government introduce a bill, and thus focused its efforts on pressuring the Liberal Party (expected to form a government soon) to pledge that it would do so when it took office. Mrs Pankhurst also sought to distinguish the WSPU from the NUWSS by suggesting that while the latter meekly requested reform, the WSPU would demand action: 'Deeds, not words' thus became the WSPU motto (Rosen, 1974: 30).

Billington-Greig, Teresa (1877–1964): An ILP organizer who also became one of the WSPU's first organizers. She was one of the leaders of the revolt against the Pankhursts when they broke with the ILP, and became a leader of the Women's Freedom League.

MILITANCY AND THE WSPU

The WSPU was not a militant organization at first, but 'deeds' soon came to mean militant methods. Several WSPU members – including Mrs Pankhurst and Dora Montefiore – had become familiar with militant methods while active in the Women's Franchise League in the 1890s. Montefiore was one of the London WSPU's founders and from the beginning urged civil disobedience in the form of tax-resistance. She began refusing to pay taxes in 1904 because 'taxation without representation is tyranny'; in 1906 her house was besieged for six weeks by bailiffs seeking to seize her property (Frances in Joannou and Purvis, 1998: 66).

Convinced that a suffrage bill would not be passed unless it was a government measure, the WSPU leaders developed tactics intended to force the government to sponsor suffrage legislation. In addition to campaigning against the governing party's candidates at elections, Christabel adopted an older radical tradition of confrontational politics, which included interrupting political meetings. WSPU leaders justified their disruptive tactics by claiming that nineteenth-century men's political movements had gained the vote by using militant methods. Having women interrupt men's political meetings was not merely a means of pressuring politicians to grant women's suffrage; it was also a conscious challenge to male authority. But as Jon Lawrence has pointed out, there was an underlying tension between the WSPU's objectives in using militant methods. They wanted both to undermine gender boundaries by adopting male confrontational politics and also to reveal the 'brutality and misogyny' central to the existing male political system (Lawrence in Vickery, 2001: 207–10).

Militancy assumed many forms and continued to evolve throughout the pre-war period. The WSPU was originally portrayed as a militant society by the press because it used confrontational tactics that men used in political settings, but which women had rejected as unladylike. Militancy thus initially included heckling speakers, disrupting meetings by insisting that the speaker address the issue of women's suffrage, marches in the streets, and holding open-air meetings. While some militants limited their militancy to violating gender norms, others, led by the Pankhursts, committed illegal acts in order to be imprisoned. This created the compelling image of the suffragette as a martyr suffering imprisonment for the cause. Although militant martyrdom generated an enormous increase in public support for women's suffrage, it did not force the government to introduce suffrage legislation, and after 1908 militancy escalated into more violent forms: first against public property (including window-breaking) and then arson and bombing of private property beginning in 1912. The more extreme forms of militancy did not replace the earlier versions; even after 1908 many militants restricted themselves to heckling or participation in street demonstrations.

It is not surprising that historians differ on what constituted a militant act since the WSPU leaders themselves disagreed. Emmeline claimed that militancy began in May 1905 when she convened a meeting of suffragists outside Westminster Abbey to protest the denial of parliamentary time for further consideration of the Women's Enfranchisement Bill. She considered it a militant act because she organized a protest demonstration instead of politely accepting the outcome as the NUWSS ladies did; militancy to her meant resisting oppression rather than submitting to it (Purvis, 2002).

Most historians, however, have followed Christabel who claimed militancy began in October 1905 when she and Annie Kenney interrupted a Liberal political rally in Manchester by demanding that it endorse votes for women (C. Pankhurst, 1959). Although it was normal for men to raise questions during political meetings, women were expected to sit quietly and let men do the talking. Christabel and Annie's actions shocked the audience because they violated gender boundaries in two respects: they attempted to assert their right to be full participants in the meeting (as if they were males) and they attempted to force a men's meeting to consider a women's issue (Lawrence in Vickery, 2001). The largely male audience erupted in anger at their impudence and the two women were roughly removed from the meeting. But Christabel's plan was not merely to interrupt the meeting; she wished to be imprisoned in order to attract attention to the suffrage cause. Therefore she deliberately committed a technical assault on a policeman outside the meeting hall in order to be arrested. She correctly anticipated that the publicity this would generate would revive the suffrage issue. The press reports of male brutality against the women's suffrage advocates, combined with Christabel's insistence on serving her sentence of a week in prison (she refused to allow her mother to pay her fine), made women's suffrage an issue of national debate. The WSPU's membership also surged; by February 1907 the WSPU had expanded to 47 branches and had nine paid organizers (Purvis in Joannou and Purvis, 1998).

Although Christabel's militant actions inspired many women, they contributed to her rupture with Esther Roper and the NESWS. Roper originally thought it was a courageous act, but she later considered it to be a publicity stunt that would discredit other suffragists (Liddington and Norris, 1978). Roper was also disillusioned by Christabel's dishonesty in portraying herself as an innocent victim when she had deliberately provoked arrest [**Doc. 11, p. 122**]. Northern working-class women feared that Christabel's behavior would undermine the work they had done to recruit women to the suffrage movement. Roper complained that working-class women were being held accountable for the biting and spitting by women of higher social standing. As a result, some working-class women became reluctant to take part in public demonstrations, thus undermining the Radical suffragist attempt to build a mass-based movement (Liddington and Norris, 1978). Even though Roper had been Christabel's original mentor in the suffrage campaign, she objected so strongly to the WSPU militancy that by 1907 she refused to appear on the same platform with any of the Pankhursts (Holton, 1996).

WSPU militancy encouraged the perception that it had a more radical objective than the NUWSS. This is misleading: both the WSPU and the NUWSS sought votes for women on an equal basis with men. Since the parliamentary franchise required property ownership that excluded many working-class men, the demand for equal franchise rights meant that most working-class women would be excluded from voting. This did not disturb Christabel, who maintained that 'our [WSPU] main concern was not with the numbers of women to be enfranchised but with the removal of a stigma upon womanhood as such' (C. Pankhurst, 1959: 186). But Labour women objected that the WSPU's slogan 'Votes for Women' was deceptive. Working-class women attending WSPU meetings assumed it stood for votes for all women; they were dismayed to discover that working-class women would still be voteless even if the WSPU obtained its demand. This is one reason why Sandra Holton claims that the true divide within the suffrage movement was not between the WSPU and the NUWSS, but between the groups seeking equal franchise and those, such as the People's Suffrage Federation, that advocated adult suffrage (Holton, 1986).

Although several suffrage organizations used militant methods as part of their campaign for the vote, militancy was not valued solely as a means of gaining enfranchisement. It was a rebellion against the restrictions Edwardian gender roles imposed on women's personal freedom [**Doc. 12, p. 123**]. Part of the WSPU's appeal stemmed from the perception that it was fighting for women's emancipation, not just for the vote. Christabel and Mrs Pankhurst considered women's active participation in the struggle to be as important as gaining the vote because it enabled them to shed the submissive attitude ingrained in women by Victorian culture. Militancy gave women the opportunity to repudiate what Christabel called the 'slave spirit' [**Doc. 13, p. 123**]. This is why she insisted she didn't want the vote to be given to women; they would be empowered only if they forced the government to concede it.

Militant acts required considerable courage; they aroused intense male hostility that frequently led to violence at public meetings. Suffragettes who interrupted political meetings were often pummeled by men in the audience and handled roughly by stewards. In some instances, especially outside London, suffragette meetings were disrupted by bands of young males, often with the police refusing to intervene [**Doc. 14, p. 124**]. Because the police were unable or unwilling to protect them, sympathetic ILP men often served as bodyguards for WSPU speakers at meetings outside London.

THE MOVE TO LONDON

Early in 1906 the WSPU moved its headquarters from Manchester to London in order to be close enough to Parliament to lobby political leaders. Given the WSPU's lack of funds, the move became possible only after Emmeline Pethick-Lawrence joined the WSPU and she and her husband, Frederick, allowed it to use their Clements Inn house for its offices. In addition to providing Christabel with an office, they allowed her to live in their house and treated her like a daughter. Emmeline became the WSPU's treasurer and with Fred's assistance dramatically improved its financial position. With Mrs Pankhurst and Christabel, she became part of the triumvirate that directed the WSPU until she and Fred were expelled in 1912.

The move to London led to tensions with Dora Montefiore who, along with Sylvia Pankhurst, had been largely responsible for developing the London WSPU organization prior to 1906. A socialist who became a member of the Social Democratic Federation's executive in 1904, Dora used open-air meetings and concentrated on recruiting working-class women, both innovations within the London suffrage campaign. Dora established the WSPU's first London branch at Canning Town in 1906, but when she attempted to form additional branches without the Pankhursts' prior approval they decided she was becoming too independent. In the ensuing conflict Dora withdrew from the WSPU. In addition to resisting the Pank-hursts' autocratic leadership, Dora's democratic suffragism was a factor. Being an adult suffragist, she opposed the Pankhursts' policy of seeking to enfranchise property-owning women rather than all adult women (Hunt in Eustance, Ryan and Ugolini, 2000: 168). Since the Canning Town branch advocated adult women's suffrage, it is not surprising that friction continued between it and the WSPU headquarters; in January 1907 Adelaide Knight, the branch's secretary, resigned claiming that the WSPU was not 'keeping their promises to the workingwoman' (Winslow, 1996: 32).

THE WSPU SPLITS FROM THE ILP

In 1906 Christabel radically altered the WSPU's election policy despite the reservations of several WSPU (Executive) committee members (Purvis, 2002). Previously it had campaigned for the candidate who most strongly supported women's suffrage; since this was usually the ILP candidate, the WSPU was able to work for suffrage and for Labour. But Christabel had doubted the labour movement's commitment to the women's cause for several years, and in 1906 she severed the WSPU's link with the ILP. Under the new election policy the WSPU would concentrate on defeating the government candidate rather than on helping the ILP candidate. Christabel portrayed this change as designed to make the WSPU an independent women's movement that, since it was not attached to any party, could attract women from all parties – that is, it was an attempt to establish a political movement based on gender rather than class or political outlook (Purvis, 2002). The new policy also, and perhaps not coincidentally, made it easier for the WSPU to recruit wealthy women.

Christabel claimed this was an anti-party rather than an anti-ILP policy, but it was perceived as an anti-ILP act because the ILP was the party the WSPU had been associated with. When the new election policy was introduced during the 1906 Cockermouth by-election, ILP members were shocked by the WSPU's refusal to endorse Robert Smillie, the Labour candidate. At the Huddersfield by-election a few months later the WSPU declined to support the Labour candidate even though he advocated women's suffrage (Liddington and Norris, 1978). Attacked by the ILP for betraying the socialist movement, Christabel and Mrs Pankhurst resigned from the ILP in 1907.

The WSPU's new policy was ostensibly a non-party position, but at Cockermouth and elsewhere it increased the Conservative candidate's chances of winning since he was usually the main alternative to the Liberal. Historians disagree as to the new policy's implications. The traditional view is that the new election policy was part of a shift to the right by Christabel and Mrs Pankhurst in which they were beginning to view the Conservative Party as an instrument of reform (Holton, 1986). Mrs Pankhurst was convinced that a Conservative Government was most likely to introduce women's suffrage in an attempt to 'dish' the Liberals as they had in the 1867 Reform Act. Sylvia's reference to the new policy as another example of Christabel's 'incipient Toryism' has significantly influenced the way historians have viewed it (S. Pankhurst, 1931: 221). Purvis, however, claims that Mrs Pankhurst remained a socialist, and cites her continued concern with the plight of working-class women as evidence of this (Purvis, 2002). Cowman has demonstrated that even if the WSPU's national leaders were shifting to the right, it should not be assumed that the rank-and-file membership followed suit; the Liverpool WSPU, for example, remained firmly associated with the left (Cowman, 2002b).

What is certain is that in 1907 Christabel initiated a private correspondence with Arthur Balfour, the Conservative Party leader, seeking a pledge that the next Conservative Government would sponsor women's suffrage legislation. But Balfour refused, claiming that it was not clear that the vast majority of women wanted the vote (Rosen, 1974). Despite his refusal, the WSPU had so thoroughly alienated the Liberal and Labour Parties that it had no option but to hope that the Conservative Party would endorse reform;

by March 1914 the WSPU was openly calling for the formation of a Conservative Government (Garner, 1984).

It has been suggested that this shift to the right was intended to enhance the WSPU's ability to recruit women from the social élite, many of them Conservatives, who would not have joined a working-class organization associated with the socialist ILP (Bartley, 2002). Christabel admitted that she was convinced that the House of Commons was 'more impressed by the demonstrations of the feminine *bourgeoisie* than of the feminine proletariat' (C. Pankhurst, 1959: 66–7). But the need to meet the WSPU's ambitious fund-raising goals may also have been a factor. Although it spent only £2,494 from March 1906 to March 1907, in May 1907 the WSPU initiated a drive to raise £20,000, nearly ten times as much. The WSPU leaders realized that this could not be raised from working-class women. Emmeline Pethick-Lawrence wrote privately in July 1907 of the importance of 'widening our circle of supporters' to include women of 'good position' who could be appealed to for money (Rosen, 1974: 86). WSPU organizers – many of whom were originally socialists – found themselves pressured to suppress their convictions in order not to offend well-to-do Conservative WSPU supporters. Even Mrs Pankhurst's youngest daughter, Adela, failed in this regard, and this was one of the reasons why she was dropped from the WSPU and encouraged to emigrate to Australia (Liddington, 2006).

This attempt to change the WSPU's class basis was sufficiently successful that working-class women began to feel uncomfortable in the WSPU headquarters. When Alice Milne came down from Manchester in October 1906 she found the London headquarters 'full of fashionable ladies in silks and satins' in sharp contrast to the Manchester office (Liddington and Norris, 1978: 206). Some working-class women began referring to the WSPU as 'the Society Woman's Political Union' (Holton, 1986: 37). As a result of this change, Liddington suggests that two distinct WSPU's were emerging by the autumn of 1907: the working-class 'community suffragettes' of Scotland and the north of England and the affluent suffragettes of London and the Home Counties (Liddington, 2006: 164).

When the WSPU separated itself from the ILP Christabel and Emmeline announced that WSPU members were to end all party political work until suffrage was obtained, and in September 1906 Mrs Pankhurst announced that all members would be required to sign a pledge to this effect (Rosen, 1974: 91). Since many WSPU members also belonged to the ILP, some historians assumed that the new election policy meant an end to their dual membership. This issue has stimulated considerable research, most of which suggests that this assumption is false.

There is no uncertainty about the WSPU's membership during its early years: it was drawn largely from working-class women who belonged to the

ILP. Despite the shift towards the right by Christabel and Mrs Pankhurst in 1906–07, many women who belonged to both the ILP and the WSPU continued to be active in both groups even after 1907. This was true in Glasgow and some other areas of Scotland, Liverpool, parts of Yorkshire, and even in some London branches, such as Wimbledon (Cowman, 2002b; Liddington, 2006). WSPU branches did not passively accept instructions from London headquarters; on this as well as other issues they modified national policies to fit local conditions. As Cowman has noted, branches did not exist solely for the purpose of 'subverting the decisions of their national parent bodies', but their independence on this and other policies indicates they had a surprising degree of autonomy (Cowman, 2002a: 300).

Some WSPU members who were Labour Party supporters resisted the Pankhursts' split from the labour movement. Eager to work for both suffrage and the Labour movement, Teresa Billington-Greig drafted a constitution for consideration by the 1907 WSPU annual conference that would have established a democratic organization in which the elected delegates to the annual conference would have had the right to vote on policy changes, such as the split with the ILP. Mrs Pankhurst responded by cancelling the annual meeting, tearing up the constitution, and insisting the WSPU needed military discipline, not democracy. Billington-Greig was furious that a movement demanding an extension of the suffrage would deny voting rights to its own members: 'I do not believe that a dictatorship can be right even if it is . . . a dictatorship of angels . . .' (Liddington and Norris, 1978: 209).

THE WOMEN'S FREEDOM LEAGUE ESTABLISHED

Despard, Charlotte (1844–1939): A WSPU member who withdrew when it broke with the ILP. One of the founders of the Women's Freedom League, she became its first President.

WSPU Executive Committee members Billington-Greig, **Charlotte Despard**, and Edith How-Martyn responded to Mrs Pankhurst's action by forming the Women's Freedom League in November 1907. About one-fifth of the WSPU members followed them, including many working-class women, such as Hannah Mitchell, who did not wish to break with the Labour Party. Although this used to be portrayed as a straightforward left–right split with the Labour activists joining the WFL, it now appears that there were large numbers of ILP women in both groups after 1907. But while the WSPU's national leaders eventually turned against the Labour Party, the WFL remained pro-Labour. Although it had 53 branches, the WFL's membership was smaller than the WSPU's; in 1914 it claimed 4,000 members (Frances in Purvis and Holton, 2000).

With Despard as President the WFL also became a militant society. In 1908 there were 142 separate imprisonments of WFL members (Garner,

1984). Claiming that taxation without representation was illegal, the WFL included resistance to paying taxes as one of its militant tactics. In 1909 WFL activists joined with women from several other organizations, including the WSPU and the NUWSS, in forming the Women's Tax Resistance League. At least 220 women engaged in tax resistance between 1906 and 1918, making it the longest-lived form of militancy (Mayhall, 2003; Frances in Joannou and Purvis, 1998).

Despite its significant loss of members to the WFL, the WSPU experienced an amazing growth spurt between 1906 and 1910. It had only three branches in March 1906; by the end of 1911 it had 122 (64 in London and the Home Counties, 58 in the rest of England, Wales and Scotland) (S. Pankhurst, 1931: 224). By 1910 its income and paid staff exceeded that of the Labour Party. WSPU income increased from £2,900 in the year 1906–07 to £33,000 in 1909–10 (Rosen, 1974). Its growing income allowed the WSPU to increase the number of its paid organizers from one to 30 during this period, and to pay them two pounds weekly (comparable to what a female clerk earned in a good business establishment at this time). Its journal, *Votes for Women*, begun in 1907, reached its peak circulation of about 40,000 copies weekly in 1909–10 (Tusan, 2005).

The suffrage campaign became a mass movement by 1910 primarily because of the growth in the WSPU (and NUWSS) branches. The branches were crucial in politicizing women and drawing them into the suffrage campaign at the local level. The factors attracting women into a particular branch were usually women's friendship networks and political party loyalties (most WSPU members had ties with either the ILP or the Conservative Party while Liberal women tended to be active in the NUWSS) rather than the national organization's policies. Prior to 1910 it was not unusual for WSPU and NUWSS branches in the same city to cooperate, and for women to belong to the local branch of both organizations (Hannam in Purvis and Holton, 2000). Although the WSPU's organizers were appointed by the national leaders and were responsible for communicating their policy to the branches, the latter were surprisingly independent of the London headquarters. According to Sylvia Pankhurst, the WSPU's national leaders tended to ignore the branches except when they wanted to explain a policy or request workers and thus there was plenty of room for local autonomy (S. Pankhurst, 1931).

The Liverpool WSPU branch, for example, was established in 1906 by working-class and socialist women unhappy with the Liverpool Women's Suffrage Society's undemocratic procedures and unwillingness to actively recruit working-class women. Instead of holding 'At Homes' in the drawing rooms of wealthy women, the Liverpool WSPU held open-air meetings, including lunchtime meetings at the gates of local factories with a large female workforce. One of the Liverpool branch's most striking characteristics was its independence from the National WSPU's authority. Acting against the National WSPU's instructions, the local women opened a suffrage shop in which they sold a variety of items in the WSPU colours – such as badges and scarves – in addition to WSPU publications. When the National WSPU attempted to draw more middle-class women into the Liverpool branch by instructing it to hold drawing room meetings during the winter, the initiative failed due to the refusal of local ladies to offer their drawing room and the disinterest of the local WSPU members in the scheme. Despite Christabel's 1913 proclamation that a sex-war had broken out and her insistence that WSPU members avoid working with men, Cowman found no evidence that the Liverpool branch made any attempt to implement this new policy; if anything, it worked more closely with sympathetic males (Cowman, 2004).

The Huddersfield branch is another important example. Although a Huddersfield NUWSS society had existed since 1904, a WSPU branch was established in January 1907. Its members appear to have been mainly working-class women with a background in the region's socialist culture. Given its class and political make up, the branch might have been expected to have joined the Women's Freedom League in 1907, but instead it remained loyal to Mrs Pankhurst. Since Mary Gawthorpe – who remained in the WSPU – was well known in Huddersfield, whereas the WFL leaders were not, this may be another example of how women's local friendship networks were often more important than the policies of London-based organizations (Cowman, 2002a: 303–4). Since the Huddersfield branch members were mostly working-class women, and they lacked wealthy supporters, the branch's activities were frequently restricted by its lack of funds. The WSPU's national leaders did not always fully appreciate this. When only 24 Huddersfield women pledged to come to the WSPU's June 1908 national demonstration in London (instead of the 200 expected by the London headquarters), the National WSPU established a fund to pay travel expenses for the Huddersfield women, but even then only 60 were able to attend (Cowman, 2002a: 307).

The WSPU's rapid membership growth between 1906 and 1910 appears to have included a considerable influx of middle- and upper-class women into what had been almost entirely a working-class organization. Some working-class women were disturbed by the changes in the membership's class composition, and class tensions resulted. Aware that class friction endangered the movement, the Pankhursts announced in the first issue of *Votes for Women* that the WSPU welcomed women of all classes, but that when you joined the movement 'if you have any class feeling you must leave that behind' (Purvis, 2002: 111). In her speeches Mrs Pankhurst encouraged the perception that WSPU members were a united sisterhood, claiming that the WSPU had 'broken down class distinctions between women' by acknowledging that all women – rich or poor – were 'outclassed' solely because they were women (Purvis, 2002: 140). Given the awareness of class differences among its members, the WSPU's creation of a sense of gender consciousness that was strong enough to override class divisions was one of the keys to its rapid membership growth.

SCOTLAND AND WALES

The WSPU leaders were especially interested in Scotland because so many Liberals, including Herbert Asquith, the Prime Minister after 1908, held Scottish seats. Mrs Pankhurst and others from WSPU headquarters made frequent appearances in Scotland in an attempt to defeat the Liberals. Although the WSPU was stronger in Scotland than in Wales, its attempts to build a strong Scottish base suffered repeated setbacks and it was never as popular in Scotland as the NUWSS.

Teresa Billington-Greig was primarily responsible for organizing the early WSPU branches in Scotland. Branches were established in Glasgow and Edinburgh in 1906, and in Aberdeen early in 1907. Because Billington-Greig had previously worked as an ILP organizer, the WSPU's original Scottish members were often part of the Scottish labour movement. ILP women were so prominent in the Scottish WSPU branches that they were sometimes mistaken for an ILP organization. Scottish WSPU members resisted the Pankhursts' orders not to support Labour candidates, and many of the WSPU's Scottish branches followed Billington-Greig into the WFL where they continued to work for suffrage and for Labour (Holton, 1986).

Helen Fraser was chiefly responsible for rebuilding the WSPU in Scotland during 1908. Under her guidance a Scottish Women's Social and Political Union was established with its own Council and treasury, and plans were made to publish a Scottish edition of *Votes for Women* (Rosen, 1974). But the Pankhursts became alarmed when the independent Scottish WSPU emerged and Fraser was reined in. She resigned from the WSPU later in 1908, and joined the NUWSS. Although Scottish branches continued, this marked the end of the experiment with a semi-autonomous Scottish WSPU. The WSPU leaders sent English organizers to Scotland in 1909 to re-establish their control (Leneman, 1991). Scots women did not welcome this display of English authority, however; some made it clear they would prefer a Scotswoman. Christabel privately described the Scottish WSPU members as a 'cantankerous' group who English organizers found difficult to please (Crawford, 2005b: 236) This friction may have hampered recruiting; by 1912 the WSPU had only three branches in Scotland (Pugh, 2000).

Welsh suffragists tended to join the NUWSS rather than the WSPU. Although the WSPU made recurring efforts to establish Welsh branches, because Wales was a Liberal stronghold and the WSPU was attacking the Liberal Party (including David Lloyd George, the Welsh national hero), the WSPU found recruiting difficult. The WSPU also created resentment by importing English 'stars' to address its meetings in Wales – thus leaving some Welsh women with the impression that they were being colonized by a group of alien women.

The most notable 'indigenous' Welsh suffrage organization – the Cymric Suffrage Union (CSU) – was established by WSPU member Edith Mansell-Moullin in London following the participation by Welsh women in the 1911 Coronation Procession. Among other activities it translated suffrage pamphlets into Welsh and distributed them at Welsh chapels in London. After the Conciliation Bill was rejected, Mansell-Moullin and a majority of the CSU members formed a new group, the Forward Cymric Suffrage Union, which took 'O Iesu, n'ad gamwaith' (O Jesus, do not allow unfairness) as its motto and pledged to use militant methods to obtain the vote (Crawford, 1999: 228).

WSPU IDEOLOGY

Even though Mrs Pankhurst's ultimate control over the WSPU was confirmed by expelling the WFL dissidents, Christabel and the Pethick-Lawrences directed it on a daily basis. Frequently away from headquarters presenting the case for women's suffrage from public platforms, Mrs Pankhurst's role was that of the 'itinerant evangelist' inspiring the rank-and-file (Harrison, 1987: 40). A charismatic speaker, she used her speeches effectively to stimulate a female consciousness. Since the WSPU's objective was equal suffrage rights for women, some historians have claimed that the WSPU differed from the NUWSS in relying on equal rights ideology (van Wingerden, 1999: 102). But Mrs Pankhurst frequently used female essentialist ideology instead of equal rights arguments. As her 24 March 1908 speech illustrates, she claimed that women had a distinctive point of view, and needed the vote in order that national legislation reflect a woman's perspective. She pointed out that existing laws were gendered in a manner that protected men's interests at the expense of women's. Although she cited examples of women being treated unfairly in the public sphere, such as the low wages female sweated workers received, most of her presentation focused on the ways gendered laws affected women's traditional roles as mothers and wives. A mother, for example, did not have the legal authority to make the crucial decisions about how her child was to be brought up, including how it would be educated and the religion in which it would be raised [**Doc. 15, p. 124**].

The 1908 Hyde Park mass meeting and the government's response was a turning-point in the WSPU's campaign. Shortly before he became Prime Minister in 1908, Asquith stated that he would abandon his opposition to women's suffrage if it was demonstrated that the majority of women desired the vote, and that they and the community would benefit by having it. Christabel responded by planning the WSPU's first mass suffrage demonstration. On 21 June 1908 Mrs Pankhurst and Elizabeth Wolstenholme Elmy led seven processions of women wearing the WSPU colours – purple, white, and green – through the streets of London to Hyde Park, where they formed the largest mass meeting ever held, a crowd estimated at between 250,000 to 500,000 persons.

Despite the display of public support, Asquith remained unmoved. Convinced by his response that the Liberal Government would not grant women's suffrage unless forced to do so, the Pankhursts concluded that peaceful agitation was useless. They revived militancy, and in more violent forms. While militancy had previously involved primarily heckling of speakers and civil disobedience, it now also included attacks on property, such as window-breaking. Some historians have portrayed the escalation of militancy as an irrational expression of women's anger, but Purvis describes it as a reasoned reaction to the government's unwillingness to respond to non-violent methods (Purvis, 2002: 108).

WSPU LEADERSHIP

Although the WSPU had become openly autocratic by 1908, the Pankhursts found it difficult to maintain control over its activists. WSPU members introduced new militant tactics on several occasions without prior approval by their leaders. An early example occurred in June 1908 when Mary Leigh and Edith New threw rocks through two windows of the Prime Minister's residence at 10 Downing Street in retaliation for the brutal treatment of suffragettes in Parliament Square by police and gangs of young men. Since it was an unauthorized departure from previous WSPU policy, Leigh and New realized that Mrs Pankhurst might repudiate their action, but instead she praised them. In response to the forced feeding of suffragettes, Marion Wallace Dunlop undertook the first hunger strike in July 1909 without the Pankhursts' prior knowledge (Holton, 1996).

Christabel's insistence that the WSPU was like an army reflected a desire for an authoritarian structure that was not achieved in practice (Stanley and

Morley, 1988). The Lancashire militants associated with Mary Gawthorpe were especially difficult to control (Holton, 1996). Although the WSPU portrayed Emily Davison as a martyr following her death, the Pankhursts considered Emily and Mary Leigh rebels because they could not control them. Davison's employment with the WSPU was terminated in 1910 because of her independence (Purvis, 2002). Others, including WSPU organizer Dora Marsden, resigned from the WSPU claiming that loyalty to 'The Cause' had been replaced by demands for loyalty to the Pankhursts (Purvis, 2002: 224).

During most of 1910 the WSPU suspended militancy while the Conciliation Committee gathered support for its Conciliation Bill. Although the bill passed its Second Reading, it was shelved when the government declined to allow further parliamentary time for it in that session. When Asquith indicated no facilities would be provided for further consideration of the bill in the new parliamentary session, the WSPU sent a deputation of some 300 women to the House of Commons on 18 November.

BLACK FRIDAY

The clash with police that resulted has become known as 'Black Friday'. In the past when WSPU women attempted to rush past the police lines, they had been quickly and politely arrested. But on this occasion, instead of promptly arresting them, the police assaulted the women – including numerous acts of indecent assault – during a six-hour struggle. It appeared to witnesses as well as the victims that the police had intentionally attempted to subject the women to sexual humiliation in a public setting to teach them a lesson [**Doc. 16, p. 126**]. Some complained that policemen seized their breasts, and deliberately twisted them in a painful manner. When a female demonstrator objected to a policeman grabbing her by the hip, he replied: 'Oh, my old dear, I can grip you wherever I like today' (Rosen, 1974: 140). Some of the spectators joined in; others cheered the police on. The doctors who treated the injured women afterwards reported numerous cases of 'black eyes, bleeding noses, bruises, sprains and dislocations' (S. Pankhurst, 1931: 343). Several of the women involved vowed that in the future they would engage in some actionable offense, such as window-breaking, which would provoke immediate arrest rather than risk being subjected to manhandling by the police again. This concern appears to have contributed to the WSPU's shift from street demonstrations to attacks on property in which the perpetrators attempted to escape before being arrested or attacked by crowds (Purvis, 2002).

Emmeline and Christabel interpreted the scenes of male brutality against women on Black Friday in different ways. The event – and the Conciliation

Bill's failure – strengthened Christabel's sense that men were the enemy, and that the suffrage struggle was part of a sex-war. In her Queen's Hall speech on 28 November 1910 she encouraged anti-male sentiment and, in a warning to those men like Henry Brailsford who sought to advise the WSPU, reaffirmed that 'this is a woman's movement, led by women . . .' (Purvis, 2002: 153). But Mrs Pankhurst remained convinced that the Liberal Government was the enemy, not men. In her Queen's Hall speech she praised the men who had been fighting alongside the WSPU. Instead of encouraging anti-male sentiment in her female audience, she urged them to appeal to the male sense of chivalry. As Holton has noted, Mrs Pankhurst relied on men's ability 'to rise above their lower natures when confronted with the "sorrowful wrath" of women' (Holton in Smith, 1990: 20). Both, however, agreed that it was good that women had to fight for their freedom, since it indicated that women were no longer willing to passively submit to male authority [Doc. 17, p. 127].

Four days after Black Friday Asquith promised that if the government was returned to office at the forthcoming election it would provide facilities in the next parliament for a bill that could be amended to include women's suffrage. *The Times* interpreted this as meaning that if the Liberal Government was re-elected it would be considered to have a mandate for women's suffrage, but the WSPU regarded Asquith's pledge as an attempt to postpone reform, since it referred to the next parliament rather than the next session. A WSPU delegation then marched on Downing Street, accosted Asquith, broke his car windows, and injured Augustine Birrell, the Chief Secretary for Ireland. Following this incident, suffragists noted a distinct coolness towards reform among MPs who were suffrage supporters, and the Conciliation Committee temporarily abandoned its efforts to negotiate with Asquith. Fawcett was privately angry at the attacks on Asquith because they undermined the NUWSS efforts to build support for reform within the Cabinet [Doc. 18, p. 128].

NEW FORMS OF MILITANCY

Militancy took new forms after 1912 as the WSPU attempted to force the nation to accept that ordinary life could not continue until suffrage had been granted. Between 1909 and 1912 the WSPU had continued to try to convert public opinion, and had limited its attacks to public property. Beginning in 1912 it began to attack private property and deliberately sought to antagonize public opinion, believing that the public's desire for order would pressure the government into reform.

During the following two years WSPU militants caused extensive property damage. They burned empty country houses, a school, the tea houses at Kew

Gardens and Regents Park, mail boxes, slashed the Rokeby Venus at the National Gallery, and exploded bombs in various buildings, including an unoccupied house Lloyd George was building. As a result, it became almost impossible for the WSPU to hold open public meetings because of the attacks on its speakers by angry members of the public.

British churches were not exempt from the attacks. The churches were accused of cooperating with the government in women's subjection because they had failed to demand women's enfranchisement. In 1913 the WSPU announced a 'War against the Church' and suffragettes initiated a variety of measures to force the church to endorse franchise reform. Some boycotted their local church, while others attended, but walked out just prior to the sermon or shouted 'votes for women' during the sermon. Some resorted to arson: during 1913 and 1914 more than 50 churches were set on fire (de Vries, 1998).

Although previous escalations of militancy had often been introduced by rank-and-file members on their own initiative, Christabel was responsible for this new policy. When Parliament was considering the 1910 Conciliation Bill, she informed a WSPU member privately that: 'If we don't get the thing settled this year more drastic measures will have to be employed' (Purvis in Joannou and Purvis, 1998: 164). There is, however, disagreement as to how far she controlled specific operations. Purvis suggests that the Pankhursts had limited control over the activists who committed the violent acts, and that the latter often carried out operations that were approved afterwards by Christabel and her mother (Purvis, 2002: 190). Sylvia, however, states that the secret arson campaign began in July 1912 under Christabel's direction, and insisted that Christabel was usually aware of each intended militant act, 'down to its smallest detail' (S. Pankhurst, 1931: 401, 317). Bearman concludes that the great majority of the arson and bombing attacks were financed by the WSPU and carried out by a relatively small number of WSPU paid employees rather than by independents acting on their own (Bearman, 2005: 394).

Anti-suffrage groups were elated by the WSPU's introduction of violent methods. They had been feeling discouraged because the suffrage advocates had won the parliamentary debate by 1912, but from that point on the public and parliamentary discussion increasingly focused on how to respond to militancy rather than on the merits of enfranchising women (Harrison, 1978). The anti-suffragists correctly anticipated that the use of violent methods would reduce public support for reform. Conservative Party conferences voted against suffrage resolutions in 1912 and 1913 despite having supported similar resolutions on six occasions prior to 1911. Following the second reading of the 1912 Conciliation Bill 34 MPs who had supported reform the year before voted against it; another 70 who had supported it in

1911 abstained (Close, 1977). In August 1912 Millicent Fawcett denounced the WSPU militants 'as the chief obstacles in the way of the success of the Suffrage movement . . .' (Rosen, 1974: 171). Even members of militant societies, including some who belonged to the WSPU, thought that arson and bombing had done great harm to the cause. Although reluctant to criticize the WSPU militancy publicly, the WFL's 1912 special conference voted to oppose any form of militancy that involved the risk of imprisonment, 'excluding resistance to taxation' (Mayhall, 2003: 107).

Although the WSPU is often distinguished from the NUWSS by its use of militant methods, only a minority of WSPU members engaged in militant acts. About 1,000 women were imprisoned for militant acts, and some of these were WFL members. Their shared sacrifices created a sense of sisterhood among those who were imprisoned which lasted for the rest of their lives.

This was especially true of those who were subjected to forced-feeding. In order to defeat hunger-striking, in 1909 the government ordered women to be forcibly fed if they refused to eat. The female prisoner was forcibly held down while a tube was inserted down her throat or nostril and liquid food poured in. In addition to being excruciatingly painful, it violated the woman's body, which some considered akin to rape [Doc. 19, p. 128].

Concerned at the public outcry against forced feeding, but fearful that a suffragette might die from hunger-striking and become a martyr, the government responded with the 1913 Temporary Discharge for Ill-Health Act. It became known as the Cat-and-Mouse Act because it authorized the government to release a prisoner whose health was endangered by her own actions, and then to re-arrest the woman after her health had improved.

The Act was used repeatedly against Mrs Pankhurst; by mid-1913 she had spent 42 days in ten different imprisonments (Purvis, 2002). As a result, by July 1913 she was so weak that suffragettes feared for her life if she continued. Even though she was aware of the danger to her health, Mrs Pankhurst announced in her 14 July 1913 London Pavilion speech that she would persevere. Claiming that she would rather be a rebel than a slave, she challenged the government to make a decision: 'Kill me or give me my freedom' [Doc. 20, p. 129].

Although the government attempted to prevent imprisoned women from dying and becoming martyrs, Emily Davison succeeded in providing the cause with a martyr. In June 1913 she ran onto the Derby course during a race, and died after colliding with the King's horse. It is not certain that Davison expected to be killed, but she had stated that the cause needed the 'last consummate sacrifice of the Militant'. The WSPU had not known of her plan, and did not desire her sacrifice, but used her funeral ceremony as its last public spectacle on behalf of suffrage (Tickner, 1988).

The press's distorted images of the suffragettes hampered WSPU efforts to convince the public that their cause was just. Women participating in WSPU demonstrations were repeatedly characterized as 'wild and hysterical' even when this was flagrantly untrue. Press accounts of Black Friday implied that the female demonstrators were responsible for the sexual violence. After 1912 the press focused on 'The Madness of the Militants' seeking to create the impression that they were mentally ill. Anti-suffrage physicians gave credibility to these images of the 'Shrieking Sisterhood' by claiming the women displayed a degree of hysteria as to suggest considerable 'mental disorder' (Tickner, 1988). The government admitted to requiring medical examinations of imprisoned suffragettes in an unsuccessful attempt to have them certified as insane.

ANTI-MALE POLICY

Although the Pankhursts had tolerated male supporters until 1911, the collapse of the Conciliation Bill (which Henry Brailsford and other male advisors had persuaded them to support) convinced Christabel not only that the government's promises were worthless, but that men in general could not be trusted. Their sense of betrayal led to a significant shift in policy in 1912 that included the exclusion of men from the WSPU's campaign.

The break with the Labour Party in 1912 contributed to the new anti-male policy. In February 1912 Christabel demanded that the Labour Party stop supporting the Liberal Government and vote against them in every division until the Liberals were driven from office. When it refused, Christabel announced: 'A Woman's war upon the Parliamentary Labour Party [became] inevitable' (Garner, 1984: 46). By October 1912 the WSPU policy was to attack Labour as well as Liberal candidates in by-elections. Thus, precisely at the time that the NUWSS was attempting to build a link with the Labour Party through the EFF, the National WSPU initiated a policy that antagonized Labour Party members. The WSPU's continued attacks on the Labour Party weakened Labour support for women's suffrage, and resulted in the Women's Labour League deciding that WSPU membership was incompatible with League membership. League members who belonged to both groups were informed they must resign from one or the other (Collette, 1989: 148).

Christabel's anti-male policy also contributed to the expulsion of the Pethick-Lawrences from the WSPU in 1912. Frederick Pethick-Lawrence had been the WSPU's business and legal advisor (often providing legal advice and bail for arrested suffragettes), co-founder and co-editor of the WSPU's journal, *Votes for Women*, and one of the WSPU's most important financial supporters (the Pethick-Lawrences had donated at least £6,610 of their own money to it between 1906 and 1912) (Harrison, 1987). Emmeline Pethick-Lawrence had been a member of the WSPU's National (Executive) Committee and as the WSPU's treasurer she and Fred had been part of the inner circle (along with Christabel and Emmeline Pankhurst) that determined WSPU policy. With Mrs Pankhurst frequently away on speaking engagements (and with Christabel in Paris after March 1912), the Pethick-Lawrences were normally in charge at WSPU headquarters. But Mrs Pankhurst had become uncomfortable with Fred's desire to have a more visible role in the WSPU, and Purvis suggests that she and Christabel were becoming uneasy with the extent to which the Pethick-Lawrences were exercising authority within the WSPU (Purvis, 2002).

The Pankhursts' decision in mid-1912 that the WSPU should resort to more violent forms of militancy was the immediate source of the conflict with the Pethick-Lawrences. Instead of damaging public property and then waiting to be arrested, the new plan involved a kind of guerilla warfare: private property would be attacked and the perpetrators would attempt to avoid arrest. Fred objected that this would undermine efforts to stimulate popular support for women's suffrage, and urged instead that the WSPU sponsor mass public demonstrations (Purvis, 2002: 191). Mrs Pankhurst supported Christabel, and became angry that Fred questioned their decision. Despite this private disagreement over policy, the Pethick-Lawrences were stunned when they discovered that Mrs Pankhurst had decided to expel them from the WSPU. Although the Pethick-Lawrences did not resist because they didn't want to split the organization, WSPU members were shocked by their ouster; some, like Evelyn Sharp, acting editor of *Votes for Women* during 1912, resigned from the WSPU. Mary Neal and Elizabeth Robins, the remaining WSPU Executive Committee members, protested and Robins resigned from the committee (Mrs Pankhurst responded by disbanding it) (John, 1995).

The Pethick-Lawrences had edited the WSPU's serial, *Votes for Women*, since 1907 and they retained control of it after the split, leaving the WSPU without a journal. Christabel edited the WSPU's new journal, which she surprisingly entitled *The Suffragette*. The *Daily Mail* had introduced the term 'suffragette' in 1906 as a derogatory label to distinguish the WSPU from the respectable NUWSS, and WSPU critics had continued to use it in this pejorative sense. Until 1912 the WSPU members called themselves militant suffragists, but Christabel defended the name change on the ground that suffragist implied someone who merely wanted the vote; 'suffragette' indicated someone who was taking action to get it (C. Pankhurst, 1959).

Mrs Pankhurst used her 17 October 1912 Albert Hall speech to minimize the shock at the Pethick-Lawrences' ouster. She reiterated her claim that the

WSPU was an army that could not be effective with divided leadership. After portraying the WSPU's campaign as a moral movement to free half the human race, she urged the women to commit militant acts, including attacks on private property, and concluded with the dramatic announcement: 'I incite this meeting to rebellion' [Doc. 21, p. 129].

In the following months Mrs Pankhurst encouraged WSPU members to view themselves as guerilla fighters engaged in a civil war to win women's political rights. In January 1913 she sent a letter to all WSPU members insisting that engaging in some form of militant action was a 'moral obligation' and that those who refrained shared the government's responsibility for the crime against women: 'Submission under such circumstances will itself be a crime' (Purvis, 2002: 207).

The WSPU's anti-male sentiment hampered efforts to work within the existing political system. In November 1912 George Lansbury resigned his parliamentary seat in London's East End in protest against the Labour Party's unwillingness to give priority to women's suffrage, and then campaigned for re-election on the sole issue of votes for women. The WSPU pledged its full support, but its ineptness reduced his chance of success. Public criticism of the Labour Party by Grace Roe, the WSPU's organizer, offended the mainly working-class electorate, and generated continuing friction with the local Labour Party. This culminated with the WSPU and the Labour Party refusing to work with each other on election day. The local Labour Party, which lacked cars to transport Lansbury supporters to the polls, refused to provide the WSPU staff with the voting lists which contained the names and addresses of eligible voters, while the WSPU, which had numerous cars available, refused to allow the men to use them claiming: 'Mrs. Pankhurst would never allow the Union [WSPU] to work under the men' (S. Pankhurst, 1931: 426)! What was intended as a referendum demonstrating working-class support for women's suffrage instead resulted in a prominent parliamentary suffrage spokesman losing his seat. This reinforced Christabel's conviction that the male electorate could not be relied on to help secure women's enfranchisement, and that therefore it was pointless to continue to try to win over public opinion.

SEX-WAR

After Lansbury's defeat Christabel refused to work with men's organizations and portrayed the campaign as a sex-war against men rather than a struggle with the Liberal Government. Although the anti-suffragists had been claiming the suffrage campaign was part of a sex-war by women against men, the NUWSS leaders – realizing that they needed the support of male voters and an all-male Parliament in order to gain the vote – had gone to great lengths to try to discredit this view of the campaign [**Doc. 9, p. 121**]. The NUWSS leaders were thus dismayed when Christabel began to portray the resistance to women's suffrage as part of a sex-war that men were waging against women. While Christabel correctly anticipated that accusing men of sex-antagonism towards women would strengthen the WSPU by attracting new recruits and increased financial contributions, the NUWSS leaders were almost certainly right in believing that portraying the campaign as a sex-war impeded progress towards suffrage legislation.

The public debate on the 1912 White Slave Traffic Bill facilitated the transition to the new approach by drawing attention to male sexual exploitation of women. By portraying itself as leading a moral crusade to defend women against male lust, the WSPU sought to revive its falling membership, increase its revenues, and claim the moral authority to resist male power.

Christabel presented the new ideology in a series of articles in 1913 that were republished in pamphlet form as *The Great Scourge and How to End It*. She suggested that male objections to women's suffrage reflected a concern that it would end their sexual exploitation of women. Men feared that enfranchised women would have the power to end prostitution and the sexual abuse of women. Christabel claimed (inaccurately) that 75 to 80 per cent of men were infected with venereal disease before marriage, and concluded that women should avoid sexual relations with men. She portrayed the suffrage movement as a revolt against the system that treated women as the 'sex slaves of men' and demanded: 'Votes for women and chastity for men' (Kent, 1987: 205) [**Doc. 22, p. 130**].

Jane Marcus suggests Christabel's attempt to stimulate 'sex hatred' was similar to left-wing men's earlier efforts to arouse 'class hatred' in that both were intended to justify revolutionary violence (Marcus, 1987: 14). This view reflects Sylvia Pankhurst's claim that Christabel's statements were designed to stimulate the 'fevered emotions' of the WSPU women who were about to be asked to undertake more serious acts of violence (S. Pankhurst, 1931: 522). Sylvia noted that Christabel's new ideology enabled the WSPU to draw support across party lines and that it appealed to the Conservative women whom the WSPU was especially keen to recruit. Feminists – including suffragettes like Rebecca West – who were seeking to remove restrictions on women's sexual freedom objected that Christabel's statements reinforced the Victorian stereotype of the 'passionless woman' and urged her to abandon puritanism (Marcus, 1987: 15). Teresa Billington-Greig denounced the Pankhursts for 'feeding and flattering a sexual ideology which juxtaposed the perfection of women against the bestiality of men' (Tickner, 1988: 224).

Although only women could join the WSPU, prior to 1913 it had numerous male supporters, some of whom made important contributions to the

WSPU's campaign. In addition to Frederick Pethick-Lawrence there were others, such as Henry Brailsford and Henry Nevinson, who spoke from WSPU platforms and who were prominent in the Men's Social and Political Union which had been established in 1910 to support the WSPU. About 40 men were imprisoned for militant actions undertaken in conjunction with WSPU campaigns; some engaged in hunger strikes and suffered forced feeding (Rosen, 1974). But when Christabel adopted an anti-male policy the Men's Political Union dissolved and its members transferred to other suffrage organizations, such as the United Suffragists.

Following Lansbury's defeat in November 1912 Sylvia developed the WSPU's East London branches into a semi-autonomous organization, the **East London Federation of the WSPU** (ELF). Although ostensibly part of the WSPU it rejected WSPU policy in several areas: it urged universal adult suffrage rather than equal suffrage for women, it did not support the WSPU arson campaign, and it was not anti-male. In contrast to the WSPU's secret violent acts, the ELF relied on mass public demonstrations and encouraged its followers to use violence against police who interfered (Rosen, 1974).

Sylvia's refusal to accept Christabel's anti-male policy resulted in her expulsion from the WSPU. The divergence between them became an open split in November 1913 when Sylvia appeared on a public platform with Lansbury in violation of Christabel's dictum that WSPU members were not to appear in public meetings with men. Following that meeting Christabel announced in *The Suffragette* that Sylvia was now acting independently of the WSPU. Christabel concluded that 'conflicting views and divided counsels inside the WSPU there cannot be' and therefore it was best that Sylvia go her own way (Romero, 1987: 68).

When Sylvia continued to ignore WSPU policy Christabel expelled her from the organization in January 1914. Her reasons included Sylvia's con-tinued cooperation with Lansbury and the Labour movement, the ELF's democratic constitution, the ELF's reliance on working-class women, and Christabel's insistence that all WSPU members 'take their instructions and walk in step like an army' (S. Pankhurst, 1931: 517). Since Christabel demanded that the ELF adopt a different name, in January 1914 its members voted to call themselves the East London Federation of the Suffragettes to acknowledge it was no longer part of the WSPU. Its membership was small – only 60 members in May 1914 – but it was more important than this suggests because of its close link with the labour movement's radical wing (Romero, 1987).

Christabel's anti-male policy also contributed to the formation of the United Suffragists. For several years George Lansbury, the *Daily Herald*'s editor, had been attempting to forge links between the movements for the emancipation of women and of labour. Originally he sought to work with the

East London Federation of the Women's Social and Political Union: Established in 1912 by Sylvia Pankhurst. When Sylvia refused to accept Christabel Pankhurst's anti-male policy, she was expelled from the WSPU and in 1914 the organization changed its name to the East London Federation of the Suffragettes.

WSPU. But Christabel rejected an alliance between the WSPU and any part of the labour movement that included men: 'The great need of this time is for women to stand and to act alone . . .' (Shepherd, 2002: 157).

Rebuffed, Lansbury and the others who shared his desire to link the women's and the labour movements responded by establishing the United Suffragists (US) in February 1914. Its formation marked an important departure in the suffrage campaign. It was inclusive in that it was open to men and women, militants or non-militants, and it resurrected the passive forms of militancy (such as heckling at public meetings and holding mass demonstrations) that labour organizations commonly used (Cowman in Joannou and Purvis, 1998: 86). Many of its founders were prominent WSPU members who had been expelled or resigned as a result of Christabel's policies. In addition to Lansbury, these included the Pethick-Lawrences, Evelyn Sharp, Henry Nevinson, Henry Harben, Barbara Ayrton Gould and her spouse, Gerald (the *Daily Herald*'s publisher), and Hertha Ayrton, who had been one of the WSPU's most important financial backers (Rosen, 1974).

The United Suffragists worked with Sylvia's ELF in London's East End to develop working-class support. Although London remained the US's main membership base, it quickly established regional branches in Amersham, Edinburgh and Stroud. Several Scottish WSPU branches – against the national WSPU's wishes – gave the US speakers such a warm welcome as to suggest that the Pankhursts could not take their continued loyalty for granted. By August 1914 the United Suffragists appeared to be successfully linking the suffrage movement with the socialist and radical labour campaign that was developing into a mass movement just before the First World War began (Holton, 1986).

WSPU membership appears to have fluctuated considerably after the more violent militancy was introduced in 1912. Some of its most dedicated members, including Mary Blathwayt, resigned in protest, but the violent militancy drew a new cohort of young women into the WSPU (Liddington, 2006: 246). While some branches, such as the Liverpool WSPU, continued to thrive until the First World War, the national organization appears to have been struggling for survival (Cowman, 2004). In January 1914 Beatrice Harraden, a prominent WSPU member, wrote to Christabel expressing concern at the WSPU's dwindling band of activists, and claiming that some of the branches had become 'half comatose' (Purvis, 2002: 250; Pugh, 2001: 291). Although membership records no longer exist, it appears that WSPU membership and income declined significantly in 1913. New subscriptions fell from 4,459 in 1909–10 to only 923 during the first eight months of 1913 (the WSPU ceased publishing the figures at this point) (Pugh, 2000: 210).

The police restrictions on the WSPU's activities contributed to its decline. After the police raided WSPU headquarters in 1912 and seized its funds, it was forced underground and struggled to survive as an organization. During 1913 the WSPU's London headquarters was raided again, its chief office staff arrested, its records seized, an attempt was made to stop publication of *The Suffragette* (it was produced by another printer but its distribution was severely restricted), and the London parks and most London meeting halls were closed to WSPU speakers. Since the WSPU's main sources of income had come from the pledges made in public meetings and *The Suffragette* sales, it is not surprising that in June 1914 Mrs Pankhurst was privately making desperate pleas for funds. Even when supporters were willing, it became increasingly difficult to make donations because in 1914 the police began seizing mail addressed to the WSPU's London headquarters. Finally, by 1914 many of the militant activists were in such poor health due to the repeated imprisonments and hunger-strikes that they could not have continued much longer (Holton, 1996). Given these conditions, it is not surprising that several historians have expressed doubt that the WSPU could have continued its campaign much longer (Crawford, 2005a: 498; Bearman, 2005: 395).

When Asquith met with the ELF deputation in June 1914, he expressed a willingness to accept women's suffrage if it was part of a broader scheme, such as the one eventually adopted in 1918 [**Doc. 23, p. 131**]. With a general election expected no later than 1915, and aware that continued resistance might tip enough Liberal voters into the Labour camp to permit a Conservative victory, Asquith's statement and the subsequent negotiations by Lloyd George suggest the Liberal Government may have been moving towards an adult-suffrage reform bill (Holton, 1986). But the cessation of militancy was the precondition for any further movement in this direction, and Christabel refused to consider it until after the government introduced a women's suffrage bill. The resulting deadlock would have prevented further progress towards reform if it had not been broken by the First World War.

As Sandra Holton has pointed out, during the last years before the war the WSPU gave priority to maintaining militancy over gaining the vote (Holton in Smith, 1990: 18–19). The struggle against the Liberals had become a kind of holy war, so important that it could not be called off even if continuing it prevented suffrage reform. This preoccupation with the struggle distinguished the WSPU campaign from that by the NUWSS, which remained focused on obtaining women's suffrage.

When the principle of women's suffrage was conceded in 1918 the Pankhursts insisted the WSPU's campaign had been responsible. Constitutional suffragists disagreed. Eleanor Rathbone claimed that 'militancy . . . came within an inch of wrecking the suffrage movement, perhaps for a generation' and that the outbreak of the war had saved it from destruction by the WSPU (Rathbone in Strachey, 1936: 24).

Historians are also sceptical of WSPU claims that its resort to violence forced the government to concede women's suffrage. Liddington and Norris suggest that militant acts 'only attracted public interest, never mass support' (Liddington and Norris, 1978: 210). Harrison and Tickner agree with Rover that suffragette violence after 1912 was 'inadequate to coerce the government but sufficiently destructive to antagonize public opinion' (Rover, 1967: 92). Holton concludes that the final stage of militancy involved a 'fundamental failure of political strategy' which served no good purpose in the suffrage campaign, and that it was the pressure from the NUWSS–Labour alliance that led to reform (Holton, 1996: 244). Liddington notes that the crucial weakness in the WSPU's post-1912 strategy was that it enabled the Liberal Government to treat women's suffrage as a law-and-order issue rather than as a democratic demand for women's citizenship rights. Once the efforts by the WSPU 'mice' to avoid arrest became the central story, the demand for women's enfranchisement ceased to be the focus of public and parliamentary attention (Liddington, 2006: 314). At the end of the pre-war period the WSPU was thus in the unfortunate position of being able to block further progress towards enfranchising women, but lacking the power to obtain that reform.

5

The NUWSS–Labour Alliance, 1910–14

The NUWSS and the WSPU moved in opposite directions between 1910 and 1914. While the WSPU's social base was narrowing and its politics becoming increasingly Conservative, the NUWSS became a mass movement with formal ties to the Labour Party. Although the NUWSS was primarily a *bourgeois* women's organization in its early years, after 1910 its support from working-class women increased significantly. The NUWSS expanded dramatically during the period, growing from 210 affiliated societies in 1910 to over 500 by July 1914, and from 21,571 members in 1910 to over 100,000 members or Friends of Women's Suffrage in 1914. Its annual revenues increased from £5,500 in 1910 to over £45,000 in 1914 (Hume, 1982).

By 1910 a majority of the House of Commons supported women's suffrage, but party differences as to what form it should take blocked legislation. Conservatives supported equal suffrage rights, but Liberals opposed this because those enfranchised would be propertied women who would likely vote Conservative. Liberals preferred to include women in a measure which would expand the male electorate, but Conservatives resisted this since the new voters would be mainly Liberal or Labour supporters. The Conciliation Committee was established in 1910 to draft a bill acceptable to both Liberals and Conservatives. Chaired by the Earl of Lytton, a Conservative and the brother of the WSPU militant, Lady Constance Lytton, the committee included 54 MPs from all parties and was supported by both the NUWSS and the WSPU.

THE CONCILIATION BILL

The Conciliation Committee drafted a very narrow bill intended to give the parliamentary vote to those women who were local government electors.

Because it restricted the vote primarily to unmarried women householders, it would have enfranchised only about one million women. Fearful that these would be largely Tory-voting elderly spinsters and widows, David Lloyd George and Winston Churchill voted against the Conciliation Bill, but it passed its Second Reading by a vote of 299 to 189 (Rosen, 1974). Although the government refused to provide additional time in that parliamentary session, it did promise to allow time for further consideration of a suffrage bill in the next session.

In 1911 a modified Conciliation Bill was introduced which revived optimism that legislation would be passed. In order to demonstrate broad public support for the bill the NUWSS urged its affiliated societies to lobby local councils to endorse it: 146 town, county, and district councils passed resolutions which were forwarded to Parliament. The new Conciliation Bill passed its Second Reading with an even larger majority than the 1910 bill: 255 to 88. Sensing victory, the NUWSS then lobbied the government to grant parliamentary time for the bill to proceed. Their hopes were dashed, however; a divided Cabinet refused, but offered a week in the next session if a similar bill could again pass its Second Reading. The NUWSS suspected duplicity, but Asquith publicly pledged that the government would ensure that adequate time would be allowed in the next session for the bill (Hume, 1982).

Although the NUWSS wanted the vote on the same terms as men, they continued to support the Conciliation Bill because they believed a wider bill could not secure a parliamentary majority unless it was a government sponsored measure, and this seemed impossible given Asquith's opposition. But just when it appeared the government would allow a Conciliation Bill to pass through Parliament Lloyd George intervened.

Although a suffragist, Lloyd George sought the defeat of the Conciliation bills because he believed they would add 'hundreds of thousands' of Tory voters to the electorate (Rosen, 1974). In response to his concern, the Liberal Party Chief Whip conducted a survey of the provincial Liberal federations which revealed that Liberal Party agents were almost unanimously opposed to the Conciliation Bill. There was some support, however, for granting all women the vote (Morgan, 1975).

During the latter part of 1911 Lloyd George developed an alternative to the Conciliation Bill: a Government Franchise Bill drafted to allow women's suffrage amendments to be added to it. Anticipating that this would grant the vote to working-class women who were likely Liberal voters, Lloyd George urged suffragists to reject the Conciliation Bill. On 7 November 1911 Asquith informed a People's Suffrage Federation deputation that the government intended to introduce a Reform Bill which could be amended to include women's suffrage, that the government would not oppose such amendments, and that it would ensure that the bill passed through all its stages in 1912. Suffrage reformers were divided by these proposals. The possibility of a wider measure of reform encouraged those who preferred this to repudiate the Conciliation Bill. Some reformers believed this was not only the consequence of Asquith's announcement, but his intention as well.

Although they believed the Government's Franchise Bill had a better chance of success, the NUWSS continued to urge enactment of the Conciliation Bill. But the WSPU revived large scale militant action prior to the vote on it. In reaction to the violence, constituency support for women's suffrage declined, and MPs who had expressed support began to waver. Even though the 1912 Conciliation Bill was essentially the same as the one passed by a large majority in 1911, it was defeated by a vote of 222 to 208. A relieved Asquith informed the Liberal Chief Whip: 'I think we are now nearly out of the wood' (Morgan, 1975: 99). The defeat was due in part to the withdrawal of Irish Nationalist support, but 26 Liberal and Conservative MPs who had pledged to support the bill (many of whom had voted for the 1911 bill) voted against it, and 66 who had abstained in 1911 voted against it. The NUWSS believed WSPU militancy was responsible for this (Hume, 1982).

NUWSS leaders felt betrayed by the Liberal Party's behavior during the vote on the Conciliation Bill; this feeling was strengthened by the collapse of its Franchise Bill. Despite the government's pledge that the bill had been drafted in such a manner as to permit a women's suffrage amendment, when it was under consideration in January 1913 the Speaker of the House of Commons ruled it out of order. This was surprising: the bill had been drafted with the intent that it should be amended, and women's suffrage amendments to the franchise bills of 1867 and 1884 had been permitted. The Speaker's impartiality has been questioned. James Lowther was a Conservative who personally opposed women's suffrage, and who had spent the weekend before making his ruling at the home of Lord Rothschild, a leading financial contributor to the anti-suffrage cause. It is not clear whether Asquith anticipated the Speaker's ruling, but in a private letter he expressed his satisfaction: 'The Speaker's *coup d'état* has bowled over the Women for the session – a great relief' (Vellacott, 1993: 207).

LIBERAL WOMEN'S REACTION

Liberal women were especially demoralized by the Liberal Government's handling of the suffrage issue. Many Women's Liberal Federation leaders resigned, and the rank-and-file membership shrank dramatically. After increasing rapidly between 1904 and 1912 – from 66,000 to 133,215 members – it is estimated that between 1912 and 1914 WLF membership fell by

18,000. One WFL member reported: 'Every bright and clever woman in my [local] Liberal society has left us' (Holton, 1986: 119). There was considerable support at the 1912 WLF annual conference for a proposal that local WLF should 'go on strike' and refuse to work for Liberal candidates, but party loyalists eventually defeated it (Hirshfield, 1990: 186).

Prior to 1912 the majority of NUWSS members were Liberals, and it had always assumed that women's suffrage would be established by the Liberal Party. But the Liberal Government's handling of the issue discredited this assumption, and led the NUWSS to change its strategy. Two groups within the NUWSS pressed for an electoral alliance with the Labour Party, but viewed that alliance in very different terms. One, led by Fawcett, saw the Labour alliance as a temporary expedient which would be abandoned once the Liberal Party had been forced to include women's suffrage in its programme. A second group, the democratic suffragists, considered the Labour Party to be feminism's natural ally and intended that the alliance should become a permanent link.

Pressure within the NUWSS for an alliance with the Labour Party came primarily from branches in Scotland and the north of England. The Newcastle Society, led by Dr Ethel Bentham, a Fabian Socialist and a member of the Women's Labour League (WLL), was the strongest advocate of this policy, and was backed by the Manchester and Edinburgh suffrage societies. With Kathleen Courtney as secretary and Margaret Robertson as organizer, the Manchester society made special efforts to recruit working-class women and worked for pro-suffrage Labour Party candidates in by-elections prior to 1912.

The NUWSS women urging an alliance with Labour represented a younger generation drawn from the provinces. After 1909 they began to occupy positions of authority within the NUWSS. Kathleen Courtney became the NUWSS secretary in 1910; **Catherine Marshall** became parliamentary secretary in 1911; Helena Swanwick edited the NUWSS journal, *The Common Cause*, from its establishment in 1909, and she, along with Margaret Aston and Ethel Bentham, became NUWSS executive committee members between 1909 and 1912. Employing working-class women organizers such as Ada Nield Chew and Selina Cooper strengthened the links with Labour. Thus, by 1912 the mainly southern, middle-class, Liberal women who had directed the NUWSS since its inception were being replaced by women who had closer ties with northern working-class women and with the Labour Party.

Until 1912 Fawcett and her allies on the NUWSS executive blocked an alliance with the Labour Party. But the desertion of many supposed Liberal suffrage supporters in the 1912 parliamentary vote which defeated the Conciliation Bill dealt the 'fatal shock' to the NUWSS's traditional policy. It demonstrated that Liberal MPs were not reliable suffrage supporters as long

Marshall, Catherine (1880–1961): Marshall was an important leader of the 'democratic suffragists' within the NUWSS. She became the NUWSS's Parliamentary secretary in 1911 and was appointed secretary of the Election Fighting Fund Committee when it was established in 1912.

as their party was not committed to reform. Almost immediately Fawcett reversed her position and began to explore the possibility of an alliance with Labour.

LABOUR PARTY ALLIANCE

The Labour Party appealed to the NUWSS in part because it had a stronger record of support for women's suffrage than any other party. In contrast to the Liberals, all the Labour MPs present had voted for the Conciliation Bill. Also, at its January 1912 annual conference the Labour Party made women's suffrage part of its programme and pledged that it would not accept any franchise reform which did not include women.

While an electoral alliance with Labour offered the NUWSS some advantages, it also created new tensions. Fawcett did not intend to abandon the NUWSS's traditional non-party position, but a link with Labour, even if limited to supporting Labour candidates in by-elections, aroused concern among some Liberal and Conservative NUWSS members that the NUWSS was altering its non-party stance. The Labour Party's association with socialism was a further problem. Fawcett and her associates were aware that the vast majority of NUWSS members were middle-class women who were hostile to Labour's programme on issues other than suffrage. If forced to choose between loyalty to their class and loyalty to women's suffrage, Fawcett anticipated they would give priority to their class interests and abandon the suffrage movement (Hume, 1982).

Because of these concerns Fawcett and Catherine Marshall went to great lengths to deny that the agreement with Labour was a fundamental shift in NUWSS policy. Fawcett presented it as a temporary policy based on political expediency. Privately she assured NUWSS members that once the Liberal Party made women's suffrage part of its programme the Labour connection would be abandoned (Hume, 1982). Marshall informed NUWSS members that the policy was intended to attack anti-suffrage Liberal MPs, and should not be construed as an alliance with Labour. In an attempt to defuse Liberal women's opposition, Marshall also promised that the policy would be administered by a special committee and would be financed from a fund kept separate from other NUWSS funds so that those who disliked the new scheme would not have to contribute to its support (Holton, 1986).

Urged on by the Newcastle and Manchester societies, Fawcett convened a special meeting of the NUWSS council in May 1912 to consider an electoral alliance with Labour. Although many Liberal women were so disillusioned with the Liberal Government's behavior over the Conciliation Bill that they were prepared to support action injurious to their party, a minority were not. Within the NUWSS executive the strongest opposition came from Eleanor Rathbone, who warned Fawcett before the meeting that the scheme risked alienating pro-suffrage Liberals; she was also one of three women who spoke against the proposal at the meeting. Despite her objections the council agreed: (1) to take into account the position of the parties involved as well as that of the individual candidates when deciding whom to support in an election; (2) to support Labour candidates especially in constituencies represented by Liberals with an unsatisfactory record on suffrage; and (3) to establish a fund for the purpose of carrying out this election policy (Vellacott, 1993).

The new policy met with considerable support. Within four months after it was adopted over £4,300 had been raised for Labour candidates. It drew WSPU supporters such as Lady de la Warr and Henry N. Brailsford into the NUWSS. It also led other suffrage organizations to adopt similar policies: the WFL and the Men's League for Women's Suffrage also decided to support Labour candidates in three-cornered contests. Although Ramsay MacDonald was ambivalent, other Labour Party leaders welcomed the NUWSS initiative, in part because the 1911 Osborne judgement had reduced the funds available to the party for election expenses.

ELECTION FIGHTING FUND COMMITTEE

The NUWSS established the **Election Fighting Fund Committee** (EFF) to implement the new policy and administer its funds. The EFF was responsible to the NUWSS executive and initially it included eight executive committee members. As might be expected, the original committee was heavily weighted with democratic suffragists with northern connections: Margaret Ashton, Kathleen Courtney, Isabella Ford, Ethel Snowden, and Catherine Marshall, its secretary, among others.

When the council created the EFF it also established a related scheme called the Friends of Women's Suffrage. Intended to increase the number of working-class women supporting women's suffrage, it allowed those who could not afford NUWSS dues to enroll as a 'friend' of women's suffrage by signing a card expressing approval of women's right to vote. Once enrolled, participants were invited to suffrage meetings and provided with suffrage literature. By the outbreak of the First World War 39,500 Friends of Women's Suffrage had enrolled, substantially increasing the largely middle-class NUWSS's links with the working class during the period the alliance with Labour was being developed (Hume, 1982).

The EFF participated in four by-elections in 1912 and succeeded in reducing the number of Liberal MPs, thereby making the Liberal Government

Election Fighting Fund Committee: Established by the NUWSS in 1912 to implement the NUWSS's electoral alliance with the Labour Party. Its formation represented a triumph for the NUWSS leaders from the north of England who wished the NUWSS to become part of a more radical, democratic suffragist movement. Catherine Marshall, a leading proponent within the NUWSS of closer ties with the Labour Party, became secretary of the committee.

more dependent on the Labour Party. Although the Liberal candidate won re-election at the Holmfirth by-election in June, the NUWSS considered its intervention successful. Even though the constituency was solidly Liberal, the Liberal candidate's majority was reduced by one-half, and the Labour vote almost doubled. In the Crewe and Midlothian by-elections later that year the Liberal vote was reduced sufficiently to transform the two Liberal seats into Conservative majorities. In both cases the Labour candidate polled well in constituencies Labour had not contested in the last general election. The Hanley by-election was less successful, but the Labour candidate's poor performance reflected the lack of Labour organization in the constituency rather than the EFF's work.

The EFF's electoral activity impressed both Labour and Liberal party leaders. Labour leaders were pleased with the EFF's contribution in all four elections, but singled out its role at Midlothian for special praise. The Labour Party's chief agent credited the EFF with adding 1,000 votes to the Labour total there and with having been a significant factor in the Liberal defeat. A Liberal Party Whip informed Catherine Marshall privately that the EFF's by-election work was causing great concern within the Liberal Party. The *Manchester Guardian* calculated that if the Midlothian trends continued the result would be a Conservative majority at the next general election (Hume, 1982).

At the executive's request, the February 1913 NUWSS council passed several resolutions expanding the EFF's scope. It decided not to support any government candidate, no matter how reliable he was on the suffrage issue, although a 'tried friend' would not be actively opposed. It agreed to attack the seats of anti-suffragist Liberals, especially those who were ministers, at the next general election by supporting either Labour or Unionist candi-dates. The council also authorized the executive to transfer money from the union's general fund to the EFF, which previously had been prohibited. These decisions strengthened the EFF and moved the NUWSS further towards an anti-Liberal Party policy (Vellacott, 1993).

During 1913 women from northern suffrage societies pressed for stronger Labour Party ties. The November 1913 NUWSS council meeting considered a resolution from the Newcastle society intended to increase the number of constituencies in which the EFF would work in preparation for the approaching general election. The EFF policy at that time was to concentrate on constituencies in which there were especially important anti-suffrage Liberals or especially pro-suffrage Labour candidates. The resolution pro-posed that securing the return of the largest number of Labour candidates should be the EFF's goal, and that to this end it should place less importance on the views of the individual candidates than on the strength of the local Labour vote and the smallness of the Liberal majority. But even some of the strongest proponents of the Labour alliance, such as Catherine Marshall, opposed the resolution because it committed the NUWSS to support the Labour Party in the general election. While she agreed the NUWSS should adopt this approach at the election if the Liberal Party had not included women's suffrage in its programme, Marshall thought it more effective to keep this as a threat which could be used to pressure the Liberals. Despite Marshall's opposition the resolution was only narrowly defeated (by ten votes), an indication that pro-Labour sentiment was increasing within the NUWSS (Vellacott, 1993).

In 1913–14 the EFF intervened in four by-elections on behalf of Labour candidates. Although Labour did not win any of the seats, this was not surprising since it was contesting three of the constituencies for the first time. The NUWSS considered the by-elections successful in that the Liberals lost two seats which they had held, and in the other two their majority was substantially reduced. Also, a Labour organization was established in each constituency upon which the Labour candidate could build at the general election.

The relationship between the NUWSS and the Labour Party began as a short-term electoral policy based on expediency, but by 1914 it was becoming more than this. In response to reports circulating within the Labour Party that the NUWSS intended to oppose Labour candidates at the next general election (due no later than 1915), the NUWSS executive sent a deputation to the January 1914 ILP executive meeting to explain what NUWSS policy would be if the Liberal Party included suffrage in its general election programme. It pledged that if this occurred the NUWSS would not continue its present opposition to the Liberal Party, but that it would not abandon its current commitments to Labour candidates, nor would it oppose any Labour candidate if the candidate's personal attitude towards women's suffrage was satisfactory (Holton, 1986).

REVOLT AGAINST EFF POLICY

Although this reassured the ILP, it triggered a revolt within the NUWSS executive. Eleanor Rathbone, who had objected to the EFF scheme at the February 1913 council meeting, led the revolt, claiming that the statement altered NUWSS policy and had not been approved by the NUWSS council [Doc. 24, p. 131]. She was convinced that it required the union to support the Labour Party in the forthcoming general election. Rathbone believed this would split the progressive vote and very likely result in the formation of a Conservative Government which would never introduce women's suffrage (Pedersen, 2004).

Presumably at Rathbone's request, the Liverpool suffrage society submitted a resolution for the next council meeting seeking to prevent the EFF from working in any constituency where the outcome would likely be the election of a Conservative candidate. Within the NUWSS executive Catherine Marshall led the resistance to the Liverpool resolution, recognizing that it would mortally weaken the EFF. While she acknowledged that a Conservative Government would also be risky, she remained convinced that the return of a Liberal Government with no definite pledge on women's suffrage was the greatest danger. In her view, the EFF was not simply an anti-Liberal strategy, but a scheme to purge reform opponents from that party. The executive endorsed her position by voting 11–2 against the Liverpool resolution (Vellacott, 1993).

Rathbone was so hostile towards the EFF policy that she initiated an opposition movement rather than accept the executive's decision. Shortly after the executive voted against the Liverpool resolution, Rathbone sent out a letter suggesting that delegates to the forthcoming NUWSS council meeting from societies which did not support the union's 'Anti-Government policy' meet to plan concerted action. A meeting was held and a committee elected to organize opposition to the executive's policy at the forthcoming council meeting. Rathbone's action stunned the NUWSS's executive committee. Dissidents were entitled to confer informally, but establishing a formal committee to direct opposition to an executive decision seemed disloyal; the fact that Rathbone's initial steps were taken secretly suggests she realized this. Rathbone's action also violated the principle that members of the executive, like the Cabinet, were obligated to support majority decisions. Fawcett was so alarmed that she wrote to Rathbone expressing her concern that such behavior, if imitated by others, would necessarily lead to the 'break up of the Union' (Vellacott, 1993: 326).

The executive committee attempted to resolve the revolt initiated by Rathbone and her three supporters on the executive at its March 1914 meeting. Although there were other Liberal women on the executive who must have had reservations about the closer ties with Labour, Rathbone was unable to attract additional support. By a vote of 12 to 4 the executive decided that any attempt to organize support or opposition for any course of action at the general election before a special council had been called to consider the matter 'must inevitably damage the present effectiveness of the Union's policy, and thus stultify the decisions of the Council'. A further resolution was passed without opposition calling for a special council meeting to consider the matter.

The issues of election policy and appropriate behavior by executive committee members were both thrashed out at the April 1914 council meeting. When it upheld the executive committee's position and voted a special resolution of thanks to Catherine Marshall for her effective defense of the EFF policy, Rathbone and her three supporters on the executive committee resigned from the executive. Privately Rathbone continued to insist that there was widespread discontent with the union's 'Labour policy' and that the council's action had been a series of votes of confidence in Fawcett's leadership rather than a true reflection of opinion on the issues (Pedersen, 2004).

Despite the concerns of Liberal women, the NUWSS continued its efforts to reduce the Liberal majority at the next general election, and to ensure that if another Liberal Government was formed that it would be dependent on the support of a Labour Party committed to women's suffrage. During 1913–14 the EFF increased its activity in the constituencies of five Liberal anti-suffrage ministers; it canvassed and registered voters and assisted Labour in developing a local organization where it was weak. The NUWSS also urged the Labour Party to contest these seats at the general election with candidates who were strong suffrage supporters; by 1914 Labour had agreed to do so in three of the constituencies.

In preparing for the general election the EFF was not limited to attacking anti-suffrage Liberals; it was also committed to increasing the number of Labour MPs because Labour was the only party committed to women's suffrage. This involved work in constituencies to defend Labour candidates who had been especially active on behalf of women's suffrage; some 25 Labour seats were selected on this ground. The November 1913 NUWSS council decided that the EFF should also work in constituencies 'where it might be the decisive factor in securing the seat for Labour' at the general election. This went beyond seeking the defeat of anti-suffrage Liberals, as it implied assisting Labour in any seat in which the Liberal majority was small and there was a significant Labour vote. This aroused concern among Liberal leaders since 40 Liberal seats would be at risk from this policy (Hume, 1982).

Divisions continued within the NUWSS over EFF policy, and with the approach of the general election the danger of a split increased. The issue of how the EFF would be used in the general election generated much of the tension. Although many Liberal women accepted its use to support Labour candidates in a small number of constituencies contested by anti-suffrage Liberals, the proposal to expand the EFF beyond this was another matter. With a general election near, party loyalty began to replace the anger which Liberal women had felt towards their party's handling of the suffrage issue in 1912. Holton concludes that if the NUWSS had honored its commitment to the Labour Party at the general election there would have been a 'serious rebellion' by rank and file Liberal women within the NUWSS. Certainly it is true that the approach of the general election was heightening the tension between the NUWSS leaders who supported the EFF as a short-term policy of expediency and the democratic suffragists who thought it the dawn of a natural alliance between feminist and class politics (Holton, 1986).

Aware that its attacks on Liberal candidates could result in a Conservative Government at the next general election, during 1913–14 the NUWSS intensified its efforts to obtain a pledge from the Conservative Party that it would introduce a suffrage bill if it formed a government. By 1914 support for women's suffrage within the Conservative Party had increased significantly. The 1911 National Union of Conservative and Unionist Associations' annual conference endorsed the Conciliation Bill, and both Balfour and Andrew Bonar Law supported it. In mid-July 1914 the NUWSS was preparing to announce that Arthur Steel-Maitland, the Conservative Party chairman, had converted to women's suffrage. While anti-suffragists were able to obtain names and other assistance from Liberal Party agents, they found Conservative agents unhelpful (Pugh, 1978). The growing Conservative Party support reflected an awareness that the party would benefit from reform; party leaders calculated that the one million female voters who would be enfranchised by the Conciliation Bill would substantially increase Conservative electoral prospects and reacted accordingly.

Concerned that the Conservative Party would make women's suffrage an election issue by endorsing reform, the Liberal Government appears to have become convinced during 1914 that it had to do something in order to prevent the Conservatives from seizing the issue and using it to their electoral benefit. Asquith, whose opposition had previously prevented the Liberal Government from acting, met with an East London Federation of Suffragettes' deputation in June 1914, and indicated that he was prepared to accept women's suffrage provided it was 'democratic in its basis' – that is, that suffrage reform include working-class women, a majority of whom could be expected to vote Liberal (Holton, 1986: 124). After the meeting, with Asquith's approval, Lloyd George began negotiations with Sylvia Pankhurst and George Lansbury. He apparently proposed a government Reform Bill that included women's suffrage, and expressed his willingness to make a public pledge that he would refuse to join a Cabinet that would not agree to this. But he insisted that militancy be halted before proceeding any further with the discussions. Lansbury left the meeting feeling elated because he was convinced the Liberal Government had finally agreed to change its policy.

Christabel was outraged when she learned that Sylvia had entered into these negotiations without consulting her first, and refused to consider even a temporary cessation of militancy (Purvis, 2002). The WSPU's revival of militancy ended this promising development, but it is the main reason why it is considered very likely that the Liberal Party would have committed itself to suffrage reform before the 1915 election if the First World War had not intervened (Holton, 1986; Vellacott, 1993; Pugh, 2001).

6

War and Suffrage Reform, 1914–18

Although the principle of women's suffrage was conceded in 1918, historians disagree as to whether the First World War was the cause or simply the occasion for reform. Most histories of the suffrage campaign stop in 1914, implying that the women's campaign had won the debate by that point. Other historians believe that the campaign was deadlocked in 1914, and that wartime developments were responsible for suffrage legislation. The latter are divided between those who stress wartime political developments (Pugh, 1978), changes in women's economic roles (Marwick, 1977), and the ways in which wartime culture reshaped assumptions about gender and citizenship rights (Gullace, 2002; Grayzel, 1999).

It is generally agreed that the war removed the main obstacles to reform. Prior to 1914 women's suffrage was blocked by Asquith's opposition, WSPU militancy, and party conflict over what form legislation should take. During the war all three were removed: the WSPU abandoned militancy; Asquith resigned as Prime Minister in 1916; and the formation of a coalition government removed the issue from overt party politics. The war also provided suffragists with the opportunity to support the use of physical force in defense of their country and the empire, thus undermining one of the anti-suffragist's main arguments.

Many historians have drawn attention to the vital contribution women made to the war effort as munitions workers. Some have even claimed that women gained the vote as a reward for their service to the nation in the munitions industry (Marwick, 1977). But this interpretation is undermined by the fact that only women aged 30 and above were granted the vote in 1918, whereas the great majority of women war workers were under 30. What needs explaining therefore is why, given the centrality of women munitions workers in the wartime discussions of women's importance to the war effort, did the 1918 Representation of the People Act primarily enfranchise women who were mothers rather than munitions workers?

SUFFRAGISTS AND THE PEACE MOVEMENT

When they realized that Britain might be drawn into the war, most suffragists, including the NUWSS, considered it a disaster and sought to restore the peace. The NUWSS participated in the women's peace rally on 4 August organized by the Women's Labour League and the Women's Co-operative Guild intended to support British neutrality, but by the time it was held Germany had invaded Belgium and a British declaration of war on Germany was expected within hours. Many women at the meeting were frustrated by a situation that they attributed to an inherent male proclivity for violence. Desperately seeking some means of restoring peace, the participants unanimously passed a resolution urging neutral nations to mediate an end to the war (Wiltsher, 1985).

Fawcett, who chaired the meeting, urged the women to recognize their duty to support their country in the crisis. Although her statements were patriotic, the press portrayed it as part of a women's peace initiative because the meeting had originally been advertised as a peace rally (Wiltsher, 1985).

The meeting revived male fears that women could not be trusted with the vote because they would be pacifists. On the following day Lord Robert Cecil, one of the Conservative Party's most important suffrage advocates, warned Fawcett that by participating in a peace meeting and allowing the NUWSS to be involved in promoting it, she had shaken his belief 'in the fitness of women to deal with great Imperial questions . . .' (Kent, 1993: 76). He warned that the NUWSS risked losing its supporters in the Conservative and Liberal Parties if she took further action along those lines [**Doc. 25, p. 132**]. Convinced that suffrage could not be obtained without the support of allies like Cecil, Fawcett declared in the *Common Cause* the following week: 'Let us show ourselves worthy of citizenship whether our claim to it be recognized or not' (Rubinstein, 1991: 214).

Confronted with a choice between a peace policy based upon sexual difference ideology or a policy which would increase the chances of gaining women's suffrage, Fawcett chose the latter. But while the NUWSS executive agreed to suspend the suffrage campaign temporarily, it was divided as to what policy it should take towards the war. Some members of the executive wanted the NUWSS to support the peace movement. Believing that the underlying goal of the women's movement was to gain the vote in order to help establish the supremacy of reason over physical force, Helena Swanwick was convinced that if women did not work for peace the moral basis of their movement would be eroded. Shortly after the Union of Democratic Control was established in September 1914 to work for a negotiated peace,

Swanwick joined and began recruiting other NUWSS women: Isabella Ford, Margaret (Robertson) Hills, Ethel Snowden, and Ethel Williams were among those who became members (Alberti, 1989).

But many NUWSS members opposed any association with the peace movement. It would expose the women's suffrage movement to the charge of disloyalty in wartime and eliminate any possibility of gaining the vote in the foreseeable future. Lady Frances Balfour maintained that German aggression caused the war and insisted there should be no talk of peace until Germany was defeated. Some who held this view considered the war analogous to domestic violence: Germany was portrayed as the powerful male aggressor, Belgium and Britain as the vulnerable female victims of male violence, and the war as an attempt by the international community to protect the rights of the weak against the physically strong (Kent, 1993).

NUWSS critics of the war divided into two groups, both opposed to Fawcett's position. One, led by Swanwick and Ford, urged the NUWSS to sponsor an anti-war campaign. A second group, which included Kathleen Courtney, Catherine Marshall, and Margaret Ashton, sympathized with Swanwick's position, but feared it would split the NUWSS. Seeking to avoid this, they proposed that the NUWSS conduct an educational campaign on the causes and prevention of war. Most democratic suffragists belonged to these two groups (Holton, 1986).

Although they differed as to what tactics to follow, suffragists who wanted the NUWSS to work for peace shared a conviction that the suffrage campaign's purpose was not simply to expand the electorate. Underlying their sexual difference ideology was an assumption that women were morally superior to men, and that therefore women would use the franchise differently. They expected that women's suffrage would transform society, and the substitution of moral for physical force would be an important part of this transformation. The idea of obtaining equal political rights while retaining male institutions and values seemed like a betrayal of the principles that had made the women's suffrage movement something akin to a moral crusade. Maude Royden's warning that for women 'to ask for equal rights with men in a world governed by . . . [physical] force is frivolous' expressed this conviction that the vote would be meaningless if the suffrage movement simply sought equal rights in a man-made world (Alberti, 1989: 42).

Within a few weeks after Britain had entered the war the NUWSS was engaged in an acrimonious struggle to determine what policy it should follow. Initially the Courtney–Marshall group was successful. They defeated Fawcett's proposed resolution for the November 1914 provincial council's agenda. When the council met it approved resolutions supported by the Courtney–Marshall group calling for an educational campaign 'to keep public opinion sane', for a European partnership based upon equal rights in place of reliance upon force, and for the *Common Cause* to publish articles on the causes and prevention of war. Although provincial councils could not set NUWSS policy, these resolutions indicated strong NUWSS support for the Courtney–Marshall position (Holton, 1986).

DIVISIONS WITHIN THE NUWSS

Courtney and Marshall hoped that Fawcett would accept their compromise position in order to avoid splitting the NUWSS. But in the following months Fawcett and her opponents became irreconcilable. Each side believed its position reflected a woman's view of the war. Fawcett informed the council that the British Empire was at war to preserve democracy against Prussian authoritarianism and warned that a Prussian victory would make it even more difficult to obtain women's suffrage. Anti-war members, such as Maude Royden, claimed the women's movement was an attempt to assert the supremacy of spiritual over physical force, and therefore the NUWSS should seek a negotiated peace (Rubinstein, 1991).

The division within the NUWSS was so fundamental that a split probably could not have been avoided. But Fawcett did little to prevent it. One issue precipitating the rift was a proposal that the International Women's Suffrage Alliance (IWSA) business congress meet in a neutral country in 1915. Fawcett strongly opposed this, fearing the meeting would become the focus of a 'women for peace' movement, but when the issue came before the NUWSS executive only one other member supported her. Rather than accepting the majority vote, Fawcett wrote to Carrie Chapman Catt, the IWSA president, threatening to resign her position as the IWSA's first vice-president if they went ahead with it.

The NUWSS's internal conflict came to a head at the February 1915 annual council meeting. Initially the internationalists were successful. Resolutions they supported were passed urging Catt to convene an IWSA meeting in a neutral country (despite Fawcett's speaking against it), recommending an educational campaign on the causes of war, and proposing: 'Since the Women's Movement is based on the principle that social relations should be governed not by physical force but by recognition of mutual rights' the NUWSS 'declares its belief in arbitration' and urges that 'future International disputes shall be submitted to arbitration . . . before recourse is had to military force . . .' (Wiltsher, 1985: 70; Kent, 1993: 78).

But these expressions of support for the internationalists were undermined by other developments that left them feeling defeated. The council rejected a resolution committing the NUWSS to implementing the above

Plate 1 Christabel Pankhurst
© Museum of London

Plate 2 Christabel Pankhurst speaking in Trafalgar Square, 11 October 1908
© Mary Evans Picture Library

Plate 3 WSPU leaders addressing the 13 October 1908 Caxton Hall meeting prior to a demonstration
© Museum of London

Plate 4 Christabel Pankhurst (centre) at 1910 suffragette demonstration
© Museum of London

Plate 5 Suffragette struggling with police during the 1910 demonstration which became 'Black Friday'
© Museum of London

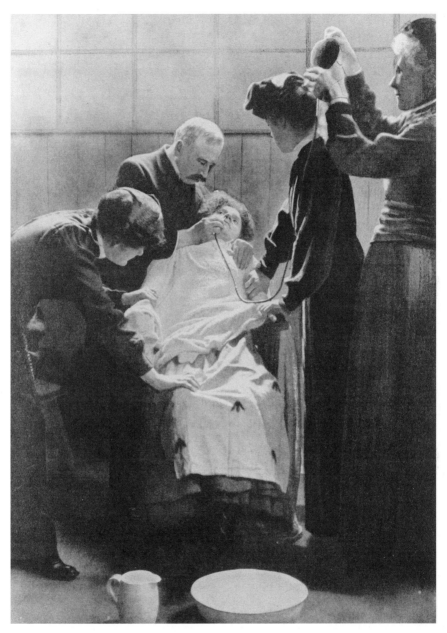

Plate 6 Artiste rendition of a suffragette being force fed
© Illustrated London News Picture Library

Plate 7 Sylvia Pankhurst being released from prison
© Hulton Archive/Getty Images

Plate 8 Emmeline Pankhurst arrested outside Buckingham Palace on 21 May 1914
© Mary Evans Picture Library

Plate 9 Millicent Fawcett speaking at Hyde Park on 26 July 1913
© Mary Evans Picture Library

Plate 10 Women's Freedom League demonstration on Glasgow Green in 1914
© Glasgow City Council (Museums)

resolutions. It also passed a resolution Fawcett desired pledging the NUWSS to work aimed at 'the sustaining of the vital strength of the nation', which her group interpreted as supporting the war effort. Finally, on the last day of the council meeting, Fawcett made a belligerent speech in which she stated that until German troops had been driven from French and Belgian soil: 'I believe it is akin to treason to talk of peace' (Wiltsher, 1985: 71).

The internationalists were stunned by Fawcett's public declaration that she considered them traitors, and the first wave of resignations followed soon afterwards. Maude Royden resigned as *Common Cause* editor, and Kathleen Courtney and Catherine Marshall, the NUWSS's most important officers after Fawcett, resigned their respective positions as honorary secretary and parliamentary secretary [**Doc. 26, p. 133**]. By April 1915, 12 of the 24 executive committee members had resigned. Ray Strachey, one of Fawcett's closest allies, was elated at their success in driving the 'poisonous pacifists' out of the NUWSS (Caine, 2005: 313). Fawcett never forgave them; three years later she described the internationalists as 'base and treacherous children who would fain stab her [England] in the back in her moment of peril' (Rubenstein, 1991: 221).

Despite the February council's vote supporting an international women's conference, at its March meeting the NUWSS executive committee decided not to participate. Fawcett insisted the NUWSS's reputation would be damaged if it was associated with the meeting, since it would inevitably involve discussions of a negotiated peace. Lady Frances Balfour warned that if the NUWSS participated in the congress she would leave the NUWSS and initiate a campaign against the internationalists. Despite Isabella Ford's insistence that the suffrage cause was necessarily opposed to militarism, the executive voted 11 to 5 against sending delegates to the congress (Kent, 1993).

The June 1915 special council was a victory for Fawcett's group. The council passed a vote of confidence in her, and a new slate of officers who supported Fawcett was elected to replace the internationalists. Ray Strachey, Fawcett's close friend and political ally, became parliamentary secretary. The election significantly changed the political make-up of the NUWSS executive: the internationalist and pro-Labour majority drawn from the northern urban societies was replaced by a pro-war and anti-Labour majority led by the London Society for Women's Suffrage backed by the southern rural societies (described by Ray Strachey as the 'stodgy' members) (Caine, 2005: 313).

The NUWSS's alliance with Labour through the Election Fighting Fund was one of the split's casualties. After the war began Fawcett changed her position on the EFF, maintaining that the EFF policy should be abandoned so that if a wartime general election was held the NUWSS would be free to support the government. Strachey, a Conservative, sought to terminate the EFF once she became parliamentary secretary. At its May 1915 meeting the executive concluded that the February council's resolution suspending all political work implied suspending EFF activity. At this point Marshall and Margaret (Robertson) Hills resigned from the EFF Committee; the rest of the democratic suffragists followed shortly afterwards. The Labour Party was informed in August 1915 that the NUWSS was suspending its EFF policy, and in 1918, prior to the general election, it was definitely terminated (Holton, 1986).

The NUWSS's decision to avoid any association with the peace movement was crucial to obtaining women's suffrage during the war. Part of the anti-suffragist case rested on the belief that women were more inclined to pacifism than men, and thus could not be trusted to support their country in wartime. If the NUWSS had supported efforts to develop links with women from enemy nations, or had encouraged an anti-war movement in Britain, it is highly unlikely that women's suffrage would have been granted prior to the war's end. The treatment of conscientious objectors supports this point; they were deprived of the franchise for five years after the war for refusing to support the war effort (Wiltsher, 1985).

In contrast to the two larger suffrage organizations, the Women's Freedom League continued to campaign for the suffrage after the war began. Aware that suffragists might be pulled away from the reform effort by patriotic feelings, the WFL urged them not to abandon the campaign: 'we make a strong appeal to all Suffragists to stand to their guns and man their own forts and not to let themselves be drawn out of their Movement for any purpose whatsoever' (Kent, 1993: 155). The WFL viewed the war as the unnecessary but logical outcome of a man-made world based on physical force; the conflict thus demonstrated the supreme importance of women having a voice in political affairs (Garner, 1984). Although Charlotte Despard, the WFL President, was a prominent pacifist, the WFL did not endorse her position; in 1917 it issued a public warning that Despard's anti-war activities reflected her individual beliefs rather than WFL policy (Mulvihill, 1989).

THE WSPU AND THE WAR

The war brought an end to the WSPU as a suffrage organization. When the war began Christabel Pankhurst denounced it as a man-made conflict which was 'God's vengeance' upon those who held women in subjection. But when the government released the suffragette prisoners a few days later Mrs Pankhurst not only ordered militancy suspended, but all suffrage activity stopped. She and Christabel developed a gendered rationale for an increasingly chauvinistic view of the conflict. Denouncing Germany as a 'male nation', they urged Britons to come to the defence of France, a 'feminine' state which they claimed was the victim of male aggression. Although the other suffrage societies joined together in 1916 to resume working for women's suffrage, the WSPU continued to promote the war effort and did not participate in the revived suffrage campaign (Holton, 1996).

The WSPU's new policy shocked many of its members, and contributed to the closing of many of its provincial branches. In light of the pre-war expectation that women would stand for peace, Sylvia Pankhurst considered the WSPU's support for the war effort a betrayal of the women's movement (S. Pankhurst, 1931). She was not alone in taking this position. The new policy resulted in the WSPU's abrupt disintegration as a national organization. Kitty Marion, one of the WSPU's most active militants, claimed that many of its members withdrew from the WSPU because they were dissatisfied with the suspension of suffrage work (Rosen, 1974: 252). In addition to being stunned by the WSPU's abandoning the suffrage campaign, provincial WSPU members with an ILP background refused to follow the Pankhursts' chauvinistic pro-war policy. Forced to choose between their loyalty to the Pankhursts and their loyalty to the ILP's pacifist and labour traditions, WSPU members in the regions chose the latter. Even WSPU branches that had been thriving at the war's onset, such as the Liverpool WSPU, suddenly and unexpectedly disappeared (Cowman, 2004: 142–3).

Some WSPU members questioned whether it was appropriate for Mrs Pankhurst to use funds that had been raised for the suffrage campaign to support the war effort, and urged that the WSPU be refounded on a more democratic basis (Purvis, 2002: 280). In October 1915 Rose Lamartine Yates, active in the WSPU since 1908, chaired a meeting of dissident WSPU members who objected to its transformation from a suffrage to a pro-war organization and requested that the WSPU's accounts be audited. Mrs Pankhurst did not reply. When WSPU members attempted to question Mrs Pankhurst about this at WSPU meetings, she denounced them as German sympathizers and had them ejected (Purvis, 2002: 283). In November 1915 Elinor Penn Gaskell, one of the WSPU's secretaries, chaired a meeting of WSPU dissidents that unanimously endorsed a manifesto objecting to Mrs Pankhurst's use of the WSPU's name for purposes other than that for which it had been established, and expressing concern about how WSPU funds were being used.

Despite this rebellion against her leadership, Mrs Pankhurst refused to compromise. Stating that the WSPU had been run like a military organization with 'autocratic control' in the past, she announced that 'that is how it will continue to be run'. WSPU members could either 'acquiesce or go' (Purvis, 2002: 283). It would appear that most of the remaining members went. WSPU members who wished to dissociate themselves from Mrs Pankhurst's wartime policy established two breakaway organizations in 1916. A group associated with Rose Lamartine Yates established 'The Suffragettes of the WSPU' which, in contrast to the WSPU, had a democratically elected executive committee (Crawford, 1999: 664). In March 1916 another group formed the 'Independent WSPU' with its own journal, *The Independent Suffragette*. Its secretary, Charlotte Marsh, had been a WSPU organizer from 1909 until the outbreak of the war (Crawford, 1999: 299). Both groups remained active throughout the war (de Vries, 1994). According to Helena Swanwick, only a 'very small body of extremists' remained loyal to Mrs Pankhurst (Swanwick, 1935: 284). Since the breakaway WSPU members challenged Mrs Pankhurst's right to continue calling her organization the WSPU, in 1917 she renamed it 'The Women's Party'.

Under Sylvia Pankhurst's direction, the East London Federation of Suffragettes became an important center of anti-war activity. This brought Sylvia into close contact with adult suffragists in anti-war organizations. During the early years of the war she began to see the struggle more as a class than a gender conflict, and in March 1916 she changed the name of the ELF to the Workers' Suffrage Federation to reflect this new focus (Winslow, 1996).

The democratic suffragists who resigned from the NUWSS continued to work for suffrage reform as well as a negotiated peace. They helped establish the British section of the Women's International League (WIL; later the Women's International League for Peace and Freedom) for this purpose in October 1915. WIL members included left-wing women from several organizations: Helena Swanwick, Isabella Ford, Catherine Marshall, and Kathleen Courtney were former NUWSS leaders, Emmeline Pethick-Lawrence and Barbara Ayrton Gould were prominent in the United Suffragists, Charlotte Despard was the WFL's president, Eleanor Barton, the WCG's General Secretary after the war, and Sylvia Pankhurst, the ELF's leader. The WIL was especially important in the adult suffrage campaign that developed during 1916.

EQUAL OR ADULT SUFFRAGE?

It has been claimed that the women's suffrage movement was moribund until the government revived the franchise reform issue late in 1916, but this is misleading. During the first half of 1916 the suffrage societies were involved in a heated dispute over whether the demand should be changed from equal suffrage rights to adult suffrage. Sylvia Pankhurst took the initiative. After a small preliminary meeting in December 1915, a broad-based conference of most of the societies involved in the suffrage campaign (including the NUWSS and the WSPU) was held in January 1916 to consider Sylvia's adult suffrage proposal. Although delegates from the Women's International League, the Women's Co-operative Guild, the United Suffragists, the Women's Freedom League, and some NUWSS members supported it, the discussion became 'acrimonious' after Ray Strachey spoke against it (S. Pankhurst, 1931: 599). Eventually the conference adopted a more cautious resolution that merely urged the societies to demand a 'Government measure of Women's Suffrage now' (Alberti, 1989: 62).

Despite this setback, the adult suffrage movement continued to grow during 1916. Some of the NUWSS branches – most notably Newcastle – were strongly in favor of changing the NUWSS's objective to adult suffrage, and resisted the NUWSS executive's efforts to restrict them to its more limited policy (Holton, 1996: 225). After attending a conference of suffrage leaders and pro-suffrage MPs in August, Henry Nevinson reported that the feeling had been 'for Adult Suffrage almost without exception' (Holton, 1996: 225). When it became clear that the government intended to introduce franchise reform, the adult suffragists established the National Council for Adult Suffrage in September 1916 to lobby for that reform. The leaders of the new group included democratic suffragists who had resigned from the NUWSS, such as Catherine Marshall, Helena Swanwick, and Kathleen Courtney (all now representing the WIL), United Suffragists like Emmeline Pethick-Lawrence and Evelyn Sharp, and Labour women such as Margaret Bondfield and Mary Macarthur. The creation of the National Council marked the culmination of two important developments during 1916: (1) the coming together of the women's movement's left-wing with that of the Labour movement (this continued into the post-war period and contributed to the scarcity of left-wing members in the NUSEC), and (2) a significant strengthening of support for adult suffrage, a far more radical reform than that being urged by the NUWSS.

While the adult suffrage movement was gaining momentum, the moderate suffragists also revived their campaign during 1916. The formation of the Consultative Committee of Constitutional Women's Suffrage Societies in March 1916 was an important step in coordinating the campaign for equal suffrage rights. Chaired by Eleanor Rathbone, it included 20 societies (three more joined later) ranging from the Liberal Forward Union to the Conservative and Unionist Women's Franchise Association, but due to the NUWSS executive's opposition it excluded the democratic suffragists working through the WIL, Labour women's groups, and Emmeline Pankhurst (Pedersen, 2004).

Under Rathbone's guidance the committee drafted the August 1916 memorandum to Asquith that shifted the basis for women's enfranchisement in a way that anticipated the terms of the 1918 Representation of the People Act. Prior to this point the public expressions of support for women's suffrage had justified it in terms of women's contribution to the war effort and had portrayed female munitions workers as the epitome of that service. The committee's memorandum began by presenting this case, claiming that women industrial workers had made a crucial contribution to the war effort, and identifying them as the group of women who especially needed the vote in order to protect their interests when the war ended and the returning servicemen were expected to demand the widespread dismissal of women workers. But the memorandum then goes beyond this to argue that the women who have 'ungrudgingly' given their husbands and sons to the armed forces had performed a form of war service that made them even more deserving of the franchise than female munitions workers [**Doc. 27, p. 133**] (Grayzel, 1999).

Although women's role in the labour force increased during the First World War, and contributed to the changed attitude towards women's suffrage by some male political leaders, recent scholarship has focused on the key role mothers played in the war effort. Pre-war suffrage advocates often used sexual difference ideology, which implied that women – because they were or were likely to become mothers – were more inclined towards pacifism than men. Many pre-war anti-suffragists had opposed granting women the parliamentary suffrage in part because they feared that they would be pacifists, and that if they were enfranchised it would be impossible to defend the empire. When the war began national political leaders worried that mothers would discourage their sons and husbands from engaging in military service, knowing that there was a strong likelihood that they would not return alive. The willingness of mothers to sacrifice their sons and husbands was important in undermining resistance to women's suffrage. When a wartime consensus emerged that national service, rather than maleness, should be the basis for citizenship rights even previous opponents accepted that 'patriotic motherhood' – sending one's sons to die – was a vital service to the nation. Gullace and Grayzel have suggested that this is the primary reason why the great majority of the women enfranchised in 1918 were mothers (Gullace, 2002; Grayzel, 1999).

SUFFRAGE REFORM REVIVED

The suffrage issue was revived in 1916 because the possibility of a general election forced the government to reform the law to enable men in the armed forces to vote. The existing requirements included a residence qualification that would have disqualified most of the men serving in the military. The introduction of conscription in 1916 made suffrage reform even more imperative. But some Cabinet members believed that if franchise reform was introduced, something would have to be done about women's suffrage. Arthur

Henderson was an important force for reform within the Cabinet; he insisted that only adult suffrage would reconcile the working-class to conscription. Aware of the strong resistance to any reform that would make women a majority of the electorate, Henderson suggested that women be enfranchised at age 25, and claimed this was acceptable to the women's organizations (Morgan, 1975).

During the summer of 1916 the Cabinet remained deadlocked over franchise reform. Many ministers, probably a majority, would have preferred to introduce a bill dealing solely with soldiers' registration. This was blocked by Henderson and Lord Robert Cecil, who insisted that women's suffrage be included in any legislation. At one point they went so far as to imply that they would resign if arrangements were not made to include the addition of women's suffrage to any bill presented to Parliament (Pugh, 1978). This pressure was important in ensuring the government did not proceed during the late summer/early fall of 1916 with a limited bill which ignored women.

While this was unfolding, Fawcett made it clear that the NUWSS's wartime quiescence would end if the government were to introduce franchise reform that did not include women: 'they [NUWSS] had buried the hatchet, but they had marked the place where it was buried and were prepared if occasion arose to dig it up' (Stocks, 1949: 81). Encouraged by Henderson and Cecil, Fawcett wrote to the Prime Minister in May to remind him that any legislation he might be contemplating should not prejudice the prospects for women's suffrage. Asquith replied that there was no plan for altering the franchise at present, but assured her that if this should be undertaken 'the considerations set out in your letter will be fully and impartially weighed without any pre-judgment from the controversies of the past' (Holton, 1986: 146). Fawcett recognized that the opportunity for reform had emerged, and ordered the NUWSS into action. Ministers were soon inundated with correspondence insisting that any franchise reform include women's suffrage (Pugh, 1978).

During August Fawcett became increasingly confident that some form of women's suffrage would be forthcoming. She observed that public opinion on the suffrage issue had changed remarkably since the war began (Harrison, 1978). Several national newspapers, such as the *Observer*, which had opposed women's suffrage reversed themselves and endorsed it. In July the Liberal Party's Chief Whip, John Gulland, reported privately that there had been a 'very marked' change in public opinion with respect to women's suffrage (Morgan, 1975: 140). The following month Asquith admitted that if the franchise was extended to all servicemen, as some were proposing, then women would have to be considered.

Mrs Pankhurst's intervention in August threatened the NUWSS-led effort to ensure that women's suffrage was included in any franchise bill.

At a crucial point during the parliamentary debate when women might still have been excluded from the reform, Mrs Pankhurst had it announced in the House of Commons that the WSPU would not insist that women's suffrage be included in a measure to provide the franchise for soldiers and sailors (Kent, 1993). This undercut the NUWSS effort to link the two together, but fortunately for suffrage advocates it was ignored. Pankhurst's action does, however, help to explain why, when the March 1917 deputation from suffrage societies to the Prime Minister was being organized, the participants unanimously opposed having Mrs Pankhurst as a member of the deputation (Harrison, 1987).

THE SPEAKER'S CONFERENCE

Unable to reach agreement on the franchise issue, the government established a Speaker's Conference chaired by James Lowther, the Speaker of the House of Commons, to report on the matter. Given the extent of the opposition to women's suffrage, its inclusion in the Speaker's Report was not inevitable. Lowther's selection of the conference participants was crucial to the outcome. Although personally opposed to women's suffrage, Lowther wished to resolve the issue and attempted to select an equal number of reform proponents and opponents from the list of names the government whips provided him. Among those chosen were two of the NUWSS's key parliamentary spokesmen: Willoughby Dickinson and John Simon. The balance of opinion on women's suffrage within the conference was upset by the resignation of four Conservatives who objected that the decisions it was making were too radical. Lowther replaced them with MPs who were sympathetic towards reform. This may have been decisive in enabling the conference to include women's suffrage in its report (Pugh, 1978).

Suffrage advocates had two main concerns regarding the Speaker's Conference. While their primary objective was to ensure that women's suffrage was included in its recommendations, they also sought to influence the content of any women's suffrage proposal – namely, to decide which women would be enfranchised. They were able to do so through a private meeting in December 1916 with pro-women's suffrage MPs, such as John Simon and W. H. Dickinson, who were members of the Speaker's Conference. While Simon and Dickinson thought there was a good chance that the conference would endorse some form of women's suffrage, they warned that pressing for something that was too radical, such as adult suffrage, would likely result in no women's suffrage at all. Fawcett and the others present then agreed that raising the women's voting age would be the 'least objectionable' way of reducing the number of women enfranchised to a level acceptable to the majority of the Speaker's Conference (Holton, 1986: 147).

This decision had significant implications that Fawcett presumably realized. Although most of the public expressions of support for women's suffrage had focused on the women munitions workers' contribution to the war effort, under the scheme Fawcett had agreed to almost all of them would remain voteless because they were too young. Those who would be enfranchised would be primarily married women who – because of their age – would also be mothers. This outcome was consistent with the recommendations in the August 1916 Consultative Committee memorandum that mothers deserved the franchise even more than industrial women workers because they had given their husbands and sons to the armed forces. Although male politicians had their own motives for ensuring that the 1918 Act primarily enfranchised mothers rather than munitions workers, the NUWSS and its allies encouraged them in this direction (Grayzel, 1999).

Because women's suffrage was so controversial, the conference delayed considering it until January 1917, after the other issues had been resolved. By a vote of 15 to 6 the members indicated support for women's suffrage, but they rejected equal suffrage by a vote of 12 to 10. Dickinson then put forward a proposal to grant the vote to women who were either 'occupiers' themselves or the wives of occupiers. This was adopted by a 9 to 8 vote. Concerned that women would still be a majority of the electorate, the members then agreed that an age limit should also be imposed, but that it should be left to Parliament to decide whether to make it 30 or 35 (Pugh, 1978).

Women's suffrage advocates in the conference were concerned that women's organizations might reject the report and initiate a campaign for equal franchise rights. Before the report was published Dickinson informed Fawcett that it would contain something 'very substantial' for women, and urged her to persuade the women's groups to accept it even though it did not provide all that some desired. He warned that if the women's organizations rejected the report's proposals, the government might drop women's suffrage from its scheme (Pugh, 1978) [Doc. 28, p. 134].

Although Fawcett had helped shape Dickinson's proposal before it was presented to the Speaker's Conference [Doc. 29, p. 135], this did not guarantee NUWSS acceptance. From its beginning in the 1860s the women's suffrage movement had demanded votes for women on the same terms as men. Since the Speaker's Report did not provide this, one of Fawcett's crucial contributions to reform was in persuading suffragists to accept a measure which some viewed as a defeat. When the NUWSS executive considered the report's proposal for women's suffrage, Rathbone objected that it excluded most of the female factory workers [Doc. 30, p. 135]. But by an 11 to 7 vote the executive rejected her request for permission to start a press campaign for alternative proposals for women's suffrage and proceeded to endorse the Speaker's Report with only one dissentient.

Democratic suffragists were dismayed by the Speaker's Report. Emmeline Pethick-Lawrence thought that it was 'grotesque' to think that only women over 30 were competent to vote (S. Pankhurst, 1931: 603). Margaret Llewelyn Davies indicated she and the Women's Co-operative Guild would continue to fight for adult suffrage (Alberti, 1989). Some NUWSS societies, such as the Manchester and District (Women's Suffrage) Federation, initiated a campaign among female munitions workers in the north of England to alter the Speaker's proposals for women (Liddington and Norris, 1978). The National Council for Adult Suffrage objected to women being treated differently than men, and to the exclusion of most female munitions workers by the age requirement. Some, including Catherine Marshall and Sylvia Pankhurst, proposed to work through the ILP for the removal of the restrictions on women. But the possibility of generating pressure within the labour movement for a wider reform was effectively ended in March 1917 when the Labour Party's special suffrage conference endorsed the Speaker's Report (Holton, 1986).

While inclusion in the Speaker's Report was a major step towards reform, it did not guarantee that women's suffrage would be part of the bill implementing it. This became one of Fawcett's priorities during the crucial period of February–March 1917. She led a deputation from 22 suffrage societies that met with Walter Long, the Local Government Board's President, in February. The deputation pledged that if the government would agree to include the Speaker's Report proposals in its bill the women's societies would accept them and not agitate for a broader reform – namely, equal franchise. Long, who had been opposed to women's suffrage, recommended the Cabinet accept this offer on the ground that the proposals were very limited, and acceptance would prevent pressure for more radical change (Pugh, 1978).

CONSERVATIVE OPPOSITION TO REFORM

The overwhelming vote in favor of the Representation of the People Bill during its second reading has encouraged the belief that only a small group of diehards opposed franchise reform. This perception of a broad consensus for reform is a myth. Conservative opposition was so strong that the government delayed nearly two months before deciding to proceed with legislation.

Conservatives were divided by the proposed franchise reform. At a meeting of Conservative MPs and peers on 1 March 1917, a large majority opposed introducing legislation based on the Speaker's Report. Shortly after the meeting over 100 Conservative backbenchers, about two-thirds of those present in Westminster, signed a petition to this effect. While this resistance in part reflected an anti-democratic animosity to the extension of the suffrage to more men as well as to women, the 'fiercest' objection came from women's suffrage opponents (Close, 1977: 904).

While the Speaker's Conference was sitting, Asquith's coalition government was replaced by one with Lloyd George as Prime Minister. This improved the prospects for women's suffrage, since a Prime Minister who had been the main barrier to reform was replaced by one sympathetic to enfranchising women. But the new government's position remained uncertain because the change resulted in two powerful opponents of women's suffrage being appointed to the Cabinet: Lord Curzon and Lord Milner.

Conservative opponents divided the Cabinet and nearly prevented reform. Walter Long took the initiative in urging the government to act, proposing that the matter be dealt with at the 5 February Cabinet meeting. But immediate action was prevented by opposition from prominent Conservatives, led by Sir George Younger, the party chairman. Curzon led the opposition to women's suffrage within the Cabinet. While Bonar Law and Balfour were prepared to accept women's suffrage, they were reluctant to proceed with legislation if it was controversial.

Asquith's proposal to introduce a House of Commons motion to adopt the Speaker's Report helped break the impasse. Lloyd George agreed to Asquith's plan as early as 26 February even though it was not debated in the House of Commons until 28 March. It had significant advantages for reform advocates. Legislation could be introduced as a House of Commons bill rather than a government bill; this would enable the Cabinet to proceed without requiring opponents, such as Curzon, to resign from the government.

The Cabinet deadlock was resolved at a tense 26 March meeting. Following Lloyd George's proposal that they proceed with a bill, Sir George Younger and Lord Edmond Talbot, respectively the Conservative Party chairman and the party's Chief Whip, raised strong objections. If all the Conservatives had followed their lead the proposal would likely have been abandoned, but Long and Lord Robert Cecil spoke forcefully for legislation, and Bonar Law reluctantly gave his assent. With the Conservatives divided, Henderson's insistence on reform apparently was decisive. Although the Cabinet agreed to proceed with legislation, opponents secured an important concession: the government whips would not be applied to secure passage of the women's suffrage clause, and if it was defeated the rest of the bill would not be affected (Pugh, 1978).

House of Commons sentiment on franchise reform was tested by the 28 March division. Asquith moved that a House of Commons bill be introduced embodying the Speaker's Conference Report's proposals. While he urged that women's suffrage be included in the bill, he did not do so on the ground that female munitions workers had earned the vote by their contribution to the war effort as is often claimed. Instead, Asquith maintained that when the war ended important issues concerning women's future in the labour force would have to be resolved, and that women should have the right to express their views through the ballot when reconstruction issues were being decided. Lloyd George and Bonar Law supported Asquith's motion, but Conservative backbenchers were divided. Although the House endorsed Asquith's motion by a vote of 343 to 64, all the opponents were Conservatives, while 79 Conservatives supported the motion (Pugh, 1978).

SUFFRAGE DEPUTATION

Concerned that the new government might ignore the Speaker's Report, Fawcett had asked Lloyd George to meet a deputation from the suffrage societies on 29 March. Although his statement to the House of Commons on the previous night had conceded their main concern, the deputation raised several other issues. Remembering the outcome of the 1912 Reform Bill, Fawcett pressed Lloyd George to pledge that women's suffrage would be part of the original bill and not left to be added by amendment. She also requested that the government whips be applied in support of the bill's women's suffrage clause. Others, such as Mary Macarthur, expressed concern that women munitions workers who had contributed so much to the war effort would be denied the vote under the Speaker's Report [**Doc. 31, p. 136**].

Lloyd George's cautious reply to the deputation reflected the struggle still occurring with anti-suffrage forces. While he assured them that a bill would be introduced, and that it would include women's suffrage, he indicated that it would be a House of Commons rather than a government bill. He claimed that because of this he could not say whether the whips would be used for any part of the bill. He also informed them that the government would leave it to the House of Commons to decide whether the voting age for women would be set at 30 or 35.

THE REPRESENTATION OF THE PEOPLE BILL

On 19 June 1917 the House of Commons voted 385 to 55 to accept the Representation of the People Bill's women's suffrage clause. Suffragists were astonished by the margin of victory. The NUWSS had been uncertain about the outcome because the government whips would not be applied to guarantee passage. To compensate for this, NUWSS members had been urged to contact their MPs, and on the day of the division the NUWSS's unofficial whips were activated to ensure that known supporters did not leave the House of Commons before the vote was taken. The huge majority that ensued was important later in forestalling opposition from the House of Lords.

While it has been assumed that the large majority reflected MPs' appreciation of women's war work, Martin Pugh's analysis of the division suggests that this was primarily a continuation of the pre-1914 parliamentary majority for women's suffrage. Of the 194 MPs who voted in both the 1911 and the 1917 women's suffrage divisions, eighteen changed in favor and four changed against, an increase of only fourteen (Pugh, 1992).

If women's suffrage was so bitterly opposed, why did it pass the House of Commons with an overwhelming majority? Conservative resistance declined dramatically after March for a variety of reasons. Many of the Conservative MPs who voted for the bill were anti-suffragists who changed sides rather than opinions. Some shared Walter Long's view that reform was inevitable, and that conceding a limited measure of reform now would postpone more radical change (such as equal franchise) for 20 to 30 years. Other anti-suffragists refrained from voting against the bill because they feared retribution by female voters if the measure passed. Also, by the time the vote was taken MPs had become aware that the Conservative Party favored a limited measure of women's suffrage. The National Unionist Association's Executive Committee conducted a survey of constituency chairmen, agents, and associations; those who responded endorsed the bill's women's suffrage clause by a margin of more than two to one (McCrillis, 1998). While 98 Conservative constituency parties supported women's suffrage, only 44 opposed it (Ramsden, 1978). This Conservative support for enfranchising women did not reflect an acceptance of a feminist rationale for reform, but a growing realization that the party would benefit. As the Conservative Party subcommittee appointed to consider the bill's impact pointed out, the party would gain an electoral advantage from the limited measure of women's suffrage that the bill provided (Lovenduski in Seldon and Ball, 1994).

The overwhelming vote for women's suffrage also reflected the fact that it was an extremely conservative measure. Despite wartime publicity about the nation's gratitude to female munitions workers, the 1918 legislation left most of them voteless because they were under 30. Women over 30 were believed to be less likely to support feminist or radical reforms than those who were younger. Also, women who had reached age 30 were more likely to be married and to be mothers, factors which were expected to make them less susceptible to radical class or gender movements (Kent, 1993). Finally, the educated women who had been an important source of support for the suffrage movement and who flocked into white-collar employment in the 1920s, often remained voteless. Because they typically rented furnished lodgings or lived with their parents, they did not qualify as local government electors and thus did not gain the parliamentary franchise; many female teachers found themselves excluded for this reason.

Although the women's societies had pledged not to attempt to amend the bill's proposal for parliamentary suffrage, they did not sit passively while it was passing through the House of Commons. When it was discovered that many of the women to be enfranchised would still be excluded from voting in local government elections, the NUWSS initiated a campaign under Rathbone's direction to alter the bill to extend the local government franchise to them as well. At first the government refused to accept the NUWSS proposal and applied the whips to prevent it from gaining support. But the NUWSS orchestrated such a flood of letters and telegrams to ministers that the government withdrew the whips, and on a free vote the House of Commons included the NUWSS-sponsored clause in the bill (Pedersen, 2004).

Fawcett had anticipated the House of Lords would be a formidable obstacle. Anti-suffrage sentiment was strong there, and peers did not have to face re-election. Lord Curzon, president of the National League for Opposing Woman Suffrage, was expected to lead the resistance in the Lords. But after enumerating the reasons why women's suffrage was inappropriate, Curzon announced that in order to avoid a clash between the Lords and the Commons he would not oppose the bill. This seemed to dishearten others who were considering voting against the measure, and the Lords then voted for it, 134 to 71 (Pugh, 1978).

The 1918 Representation of the People Act granted the vote to 8,400,000 women, who comprised 39.6 per cent of the electorate. The Act is often mistakenly said to have enfranchised women aged 30 and above. In addition to the age requirement, it restricted the vote to those women who were also local government electors or the wives of local government electors. It is estimated that about 22 per cent of the women aged 30 or above were excluded from voting by this additional requirement; many of these were working-class or unmarried employed women (Tanner, 1990). Fawcett acknowledged that the legislation could almost be considered a 'motherhood franchise' since about five-sixths (83 per cent) of the newly enfranchised women were wives and mothers (Grayzel, 1999: 213). If it is understood that the women enfranchised by the 1918 Act were disproportionately middle-class housewives aged 30 and above, then the tendency of women to vote Conservative in the 1920s becomes less surprising (Turner, 1992).

The war's importance in shaping the terms under which women were enfranchised is evident when the pre-war demand is compared with what the 1918 Act established. Prior to the war suffragists fought for equal suffrage rights and, because the pre-war suffrage was tied to property ownership, anticipated that reform would mean the enfranchisement of a relatively small number of women, most of whom would be unmarried since they would have to own property in their own name. But the 1918 legislation was very different: it did not grant equal suffrage rights; it did enfranchise much greater numbers of women than envisioned by the pre-war campaigners (except for the adult suffragists); and it largely enfranchised mothers rather than unmarried (and childless) women.

Fawcett considered the enactment of the suffrage legislation the greatest moment in her life. Suffrage societies sponsored a victory party at the Queen's Hall in March 1918 for which William Blake's poem, 'Jerusalem', was set to music as the suffrage hymn. But suffragist celebrations were muted by their awareness that they had not obtained the equal suffrage rights for which they had been campaigning since the 1860s. Since the Act gave the vote to men at 19 if they had seen active service in the armed forces (and to all men at age 21), it preserved women's different and inferior status under the law. While few went as far as Dora Montefiore in accusing the suffrage societies of having 'betrayed' their supporters by accepting legislation that fell short of equality, reformers were aware that they had won a battle, not the war (Montefiore, 1927: 194).

7

Equal Franchise, 1919–28

Until recently historians have virtually ignored the post-1918 equal franchise campaign. Sylvia Pankhurst claimed that the 1928 Representation of the People Act came 'virtually without effort' t, 1931: 608); her assumption that it was inevitable, and accom- little struggle, partially explains the lack of scholarly attention. it women's organizations were less visible and played a less dramatic role than in the pre-war campaign may also have been a factor. This chapter suggests that Sylvia Pankhurst's assumptions need rethinking: equal franchise was obtained only after an intense decade-long struggle in which women were active participants.

Historians disagree on how equal franchise rights were obtained in 1928. Cheryl Law attributes it to the women's movement, and suggests that reform resulted from the women's groups' ability to work together for a common goal (Law, 1997). Susan Pedersen, however, notes that the Cabinet records indicate that Baldwin's Conservative Government did not proceed with equal franchise legislation because of the women's campaign (Pedersen, 2004: 195). Several historians, including David Jarvis, have claimed that the Conservative Party's reasons for enacting suffrage legislation had more to do with its need to attract female voters than to pressure from feminist groups. Conservative Party leaders recognized that women voters were crucial to the party's electoral success, and considered equal franchise reform part of their effort to make the Conservative Party the 'women's party' (Jarvis, 1994).

While attention has shifted to the Conservative Party's reasons for passing suffrage legislation, scholars differ as to how it came to support that reform. Anthony Seldon claims that there was a broad party consensus for reform with only a tiny 'right-wing rump' opposed to it (Seldon and Ball, 1994: 33). This, however, ignores the evidence that at least until 1927 a majority of the party opposed granting equal franchise rights at age 21, that there was intense inter-party conflict over the issue, and that it required Baldwin's considerable managerial skills to convince the party to proceed with legislation with a minimal amount of public opposition. Although Martin Pugh has drawn attention to Conservative Party women's importance in convincing the party to proceed with reform, this topic needs more research (Pugh, 1992).

Certainly there was nothing inevitable about the Conservative Party introducing equal franchise reform, especially by lowering it to age 21. During the 1920s that issue divided the party. Although Conservative Party leaders consistently expressed support for the principle, Conservative MPs provided 84 per cent of the suffrage opponents in the 1919, 1920 and 1924 parliamentary divisions; in the 1919 and 1924 divisions more Conservatives voted against reform than voted for it (Harrison, 1978). The struggle over the 1928 Representation of the People Bill was primarily between the Conservative Government and its backbenchers; the other two parties supported it. Since even Conservatives who wanted equal franchise reform generally preferred that it be granted at age 25, the fact that a Conservative Government reduced women's voting age to 21 requires explanation.

The case for equal franchise did not rest solely on the inequity in sex-differentiated voting ages. Although employed women might be regarded as particularly in need of the vote, the 1918 Act ensured that women who worked for pay were especially likely to be voteless. In the 1920s it was estimated that only about one of every fifteen employed women had the vote. Women working in industry were typically young and unmarried and thus disqualified by the age limit. But many professional women, even those over age 30, were also ineligible to vote. Many professions had a marriage bar, and therefore most were unmarried and unable to qualify through their husbands' eligibility. Because most professional women rented furnished accommodations, they did not meet the property qualification. It is not known whether the 1918 Act was intended to have this consequence, but it kept most of the educated women who worked for a living disenfranchised, even though they presumably would have been especially well-informed voters [**Doc. 32, p. 136**].

THE FEMINIST SOCIETIES

During the 1920s there were three main sources of organized pressure for equal franchise: feminist societies, the Conservative Party women's organization, and Labour Party women. After the principle of women's suffrage was conceded in 1918, the NUWSS transformed itself into the National Union of Societies for Equal Citizenship. Eleanor Rathbone replaced Millicent Fawcett as president in 1919, and the NUSEC adopted a new programme that included equal franchise at age 21. Several pre-war societies joined with it in the suffrage campaign: the Women's Freedom League, the **London Society**

London Society for Women's Service: Chaired by Clementia Taylor, the London National Society for Women's Suffrage was established in 1867. After several name changes it was renamed the London Society for Women's Suffrage in 1907 and became the London Society for Women's Service in 1919. In 1953 it became the Fawcett Society.

Rhondda, Viscountess [Margaret Haig Thomas] (1883–1958): A member of the Women's Social and Political Union who was imprisoned briefly for setting fire to letter-boxes. In 1921 she founded the Six Point Group to work for feminist reforms. Dissatisfied with the lack of progress towards equal franchise, she formed the Equal Political Rights Campaign Committee in 1926 in an attempt to ginger up the campaign.

Astor, Nancy (1879–1964): In 1919 Astor became the first female member of the House of Commons. She established the Consultative Committee of Women's Organisations in 1921 to develop an agreed feminist reform programme. Astor was the key female within the Conservative Party lobbying for equal franchise in the 1920s.

for Women's Service (previously the London Society for Women's Suffrage), and St Joan's Social and Political Alliance (previously the Catholic Women's Suffrage Society). These were reinforced by two new groups: **Lady Rhondda** formed the Six Point Group (SPG) in February 1921 to work for gender equality (although it did not add equal franchise to its 'Immediate *Programme*' until 1926) and in March 1921 Lady **Astor** established the Consultative Committee of Women's Organisations to coordinate efforts by women's groups to pressure Parliament for legislation to improve women's status (Smith in Smith, 1990).

As the largest of the post-war feminist societies, the NUSEC intended to become the 'co-ordinating organ' for all British feminist activity. But it emerged from the First World War in a considerably weakened position. The NUWSS's membership declined rapidly during the war's final years; in 1915 it had 447 member societies but only 234 by October 1918 and it was facing severe financial constraints (Holton, 1986: 186). With the political parties opened to women, many worked through their party rather than through NUSEC. Also, equal rights feminists became disenchanted with the NUSEC as it increasingly reflected Rathbone's New Feminist ideology and reform *programme*: birth control, family allowances, and protective legislation solely for women (Smith in Smith, 1990).

Some LSWS leaders, including Ray Strachey, were so unhappy with the NUSEC's new *programme* and ideology that early in 1919 they persuaded the LSWS to re-establish itself as an independent organization with a new name: the London Society for Women's Service (later changed to the London and National Society for Women's Service) (Alberti, 1989). This allowed the LSWS to pursue its own *programme*, rather than being committed to NUSEC's. Although the LSWS endorsed equal suffrage, its immediate objective was to obtain 'economic equality' (equal pay and equal employment opportunities) for women.

The LSWS collaborated with the NUSEC in the equal suffrage campaign, but differed on other issues because its equal rights feminism conflicted with Rathbone's commitment to the New Feminism (Smith in Smith, 1990). Ray Strachey, for example, was a member of the NUSEC's executive committee from 1919 to 1924, but by 1927 she was so alienated by its New Feminism that she privately admitted that she couldn't 'pretend to care very much what happens to the NUSEC' (Harrison, 1987: 165).

During the 1920s the SPG became an important alternative to the NUSEC among feminist groups. Lady Rhondda had considered joining the NUSEC after the First World War, but the strong-willed Rhondda had not felt welcome and established her own organization, the SPG (Pedersen, 2004: 185). It was distinctive for several reasons. While the NUSEC members were almost entirely suffragists, many of the SPG's most prominent members, including Rhondda, had been suffragettes. While the NUSEC opposed sex-war and urged cooperation with men, the SPG acknowledged gender conflict and encouraged women to become more assertive in dealing with men (Smith in Smith, 1990). As the NUSEC's programme gradually reflected Rathbone's New Feminist ideology, the SPG increasingly claimed to speak for an alternative feminism based on equal rights ideology.

The Consultative Committee was Lady Astor's brainchild. Following her election in 1919, Astor was the first woman to take a seat in the House of Commons, but since she had not been active in the women's movement (or in politics), suffragists were concerned that she would be ineffective, and possibly not even an ally. Aware of her limitations, Astor asked Ray Strachey (who was also the NUSEC's parliamentary secretary) to serve as her parliamentary secretary, drafting her memoranda and speeches, and generally advising her on how to be a successful MP. With Strachey's assistance, Astor became an important voice for women's reforms, supporting women's issues even when they conflicted with her party's position (Alberti, 1989).

Astor found it difficult to be the women's parliamentary spokesperson because the women's movement had fragmented into numerous groups with conflicting views on issues. To remedy this, she persuaded the women's societies to join together in the Consultative Committee of Women's Organisations. Some 60 women's groups were represented at its first official meeting in June 1921, including the NUSEC and the Conservative and Liberal Party women's organizations, but not the Labour Party's. The Consultative Committee was intended to be a coordinating body through which women's organizations would adopt a united position on issues so that they could lobby Parliament more effectively. It also intervened in elections in an attempt to elect MPs that supported women's reforms. The committee sent a statement presenting women's views to each political party prior to the October 1922 general election. It also set up a 'fighting fund' to finance constituency campaigns intended to defeat MPs hostile to women's issues (Pugh, 1992).

The 1918 Representation of the People Act enfranchised an additional five million men, most of them working-class and expected to become Labour voters. Seeking to widen its pool of supporters to offset Labour's gain, the Conservative Party turned to the new female electorate. The first step was the creation of a Conservative women's organization. In 1918 women were allowed to become party members, the Women's Unionist Organisation was established, a Women's Advisory Committee formed, and one-third of the seats on the National Union's Central Council and other party bodies were reserved for women (Pugh, 1992).

When it became apparent that women would gain the parliamentary vote, the Labour Party also sought to appeal to them. The party's national executive committee arranged a merger with the Women's Labour League, allowed

Standing Joint Committee of Industrial Women's Organisations: Established in February 1916 by women's organizations concerned that female workers were being used by employers to undercut male wage rates. Chaired by Mary Macarthur, National Federation of Women Workers' secretary, it included representatives from the major working-class women's organizations such as the Women's Co-operative Guild and the Women's Labour League. It became the Labour Party's Women's Advisory Committee in 1918.

individual women to join local constituency parties, guaranteed women four seats on the party's executive committee, and recognized the **Standing Joint Committee of Industrial Women's Organizations** (SJCIWO) as the party's women's advisory committee. At the 1918 party conference Arthur Henderson welcomed the new female voters into the Labour Party as 'equal partners'. In its 1918 general election manifesto the party pledged support for the immediate extension of the vote to women at age 21.

In 1919 the Labour Party introduced a Women's Emancipation Bill that would have established equal suffrage rights by allowing women to vote at age 21. Feminist and Labour women's organizations temporarily allied to secure its passage. While Parliament was considering the bill, the NUSEC and the SJCIWO sent a joint deputation to the Home Secretary urging the government to support it, and later joined forces in sponsoring a public rally to arouse support for it (Smith, 1984). The women's societies lobbied vigorously for the bill, and initially it appeared that it would pass. Ray Strachey, the NUSEC's parliamentary secretary and one of the main lobbyists for the bill, found that MPs were eager to talk to her, and she was amused to hear ideas expressed in the Parliamentary debate that she 'had just put in their mouths' a few minutes earlier (Alberti, 1989: 98).

Although the Coalition Government's 1918 election manifesto pledged that it would 'remove all existing inequalities of the law as between men and women', it was alarmed by the Women's Emancipation Bill's progress through the House of Commons. The government applied the whips in an attempt to defeat the bill, but despite this it passed its second reading in the House of Commons by a vote of 100 to 88. This was an impressive, albeit temporary, victory for the women's societies. Coalition MPs braved the whips' displeasure because for a brief period in 1919 they were even more fearful of the newly enfranchised women voters. Women's groups had made clear that they gave the bill's enactment a high priority, and MPs anticipated that women would vote as a gender bloc to defeat those who opposed it (Smith in Smith, 1990). When the bill reached the House of Lords, however, the Coalition Government blocked it, and replaced it with an alternative measure – the Sex Disqualification (Removal) Bill – that did not include suffrage reform.

Equal franchise bills were introduced almost every year in the early 1920s, but despite strong parliamentary support most were blocked by government opposition. In 1920 a NUSEC-backed Labour Party bill passed its second reading in the House of Commons with a large majority, but the government killed it during the committee stage. In 1921 NUSEC obtained the signatures of almost 200 MPs to an equal franchise memorial which was presented to the Prime Minister. In the following year NUSEC lobbied intensively for Lord Robert Cecil's Women's Enfranchisement Bill, which passed its second reading in the House of Commons by a 208 to 60 vote, but the government fell from office before it could become law. In 1923 the NUSEC secured the signatures of over 200 MPs to an equal franchise memorial presented in conjunction with Isaac Foot's Women's Enfranchisement Bill, but it was also unsuccessful. Conservative MPs provided the bulk of the opposition to these bills.

THE LABOUR GOVERNMENT AND FRANCHISE REFORM

Since the Labour Party had consistently advocated equal franchise, and had stated in its 1923 election manifesto that it stood for 'equal political and legal rights', reformers expected the 1924 Labour Government to introduce suffrage legislation. Because of their high expectations, suffragists were bitterly disappointed when it failed to do so. The debate on William Adamson's private member's bill to grant equal franchise rights at age 21 was notable for several reasons. The Duchess of Atholl expressed the Conservative Party's opposition to the bill on the ground that an all-party conference should be held before legislation was considered (which would have the effect of delaying reform). Another Conservative, Sir Martin Conway, recommended for the first time in the suffrage debates that equal franchise be granted at age 25, an idea that was gaining popularity within the Conservative Party. After Adamson's bill passed its second reading and the committee stage, the Prime Minister indicated that the Labour Government would make it a government measure and proceed with it but this had not yet happened when the government resigned unexpectedly (Law, 1997).

Feminists publicly criticized the Labour Government because they felt betrayed by its reluctance to sponsor reform. Although Rathbone had sought closer ties between feminists and Labour women, she reported to the NUSEC Annual Council meeting that Labour had broken faith with the women who had supported it: 'Has a party in office no responsibility towards its principles and past professions and pledges' (Alberti, 1989: 145)?

Equal franchise provided a basis for a united women's movement in the 1920s, but class and party affiliation provided competing identities that hampered efforts to develop gender solidarity. The Labour Party considered feminist groups to be rivals for women's allegiance and feared that they would encourage a gender consciousness that would undercut Labour's class-based ideology. At the 1918 and 1920 Labour Party women's conferences resolutions were passed urging Labour women not to join single-sex (feminist) organizations as 'they would be in danger of getting their political opinions muddled' (Smith, 1984: 24). The SJCIWO refused to join Astor's Consultative Committee in 1921 because of this resolution ('Report of the SJC for 1920–21', 1921: 100).

The General Strike heightened class feeling which further undermined links between the women's movement and the Labour Party. The Labour Party NEC intervened to stop the SJCIWO from cooperating with feminist groups campaigning for equal franchise even though the SJCIWO (and the Labour Party) continued to support it. Although the SJCIWO had been participating in NUSEC sponsored activities, early in 1927 Labour's NEC denied it permission to send representatives to a suffrage rally, claiming that the NUSEC 'industrial and social policy was not sound' (Smith, 1984: 33). The two Labour MPs who had been invited to speak at the July 1927 equal franchise rally – Margaret Bondfield and Ellen Wilkinson – both declined. Later that year the SJCIWO notified the NUSEC it would no longer be able to cooperate in the suffrage campaign or other matters so long as the NUSEC continued its opposition to protective legislation for women.

Strong party ties also hampered the women's societies' efforts to pressure political parties for suffrage reform. At the October 1924 Consultative Committee of Women's Organisations meeting, Eva Hubback, the NUSEC representative, admitted that the Labour Party's election manifesto had not mentioned equal suffrage, but because the party supported reform she urged the Committee not to express its indignation, but to simply send it a resolution urging that it publicly endorse women's suffrage. When a resolution was proposed expressing regret that the Conservative Government was committed only to holding a conference on the subject, the Committee divided since some members felt that this could lead to reform being postponed indefinitely. Some thought the resolution unfairly critical of the Conservative Party; others did not think it strong enough. Eventually the resolution was withdrawn, and one expressing dissatisfaction with all three party manifestos was passed (Consultative Committee minutes, 1924).

By the mid-1920s the problem suffrage reformers had to overcome was not overt opposition to equal franchise. Labour and Conservative Party leaders repeatedly expressed support for the equal franchise principle, and few politicians publicly opposed it. But endorsing the principle had become a substitute for action; political leaders coupled their approval of equal franchise with claims that the time was not yet right to introduce it. The difficulty for reformers was how to move politicians from accepting the principle to a commitment to implementing it.

WOMEN AND THE CONSERVATIVE PARTY

Reformers benefited from Conservative Party leaders' awareness that women had become vital to the party's future. In the 1920s the women's organization was the party's most rapidly growing unit. By 1924 there were women's branches in 355 constituencies; by 1928 paid female party membership had grown to nearly one million. Conservative Party professionals acknowledged that the party's women's house-to-house membership recruiting and canvassing made an important contribution to the October 1924 general election victory. The party also became increasingly dependent on the women's organization for fundraising. By the end of the 1920s the women's branches were raising the greater proportion of the money used to finance Conservative constituency associations, and party leaders were urging Conservative men to try to keep up with the women (Jarvis, 1996).

Women voters were also crucial to the Conservative Party's electoral success in the 1920s. During that decade women were more likely than men to vote Conservative; the higher the proportion of women in a constituency, the less well the Labour candidate tended to do (Rasmussen, 1984). Conservative voting in the 1924 general election tended to rise in proportion to the number of female voters in the constituency; in those constituencies where women comprised more than 40 per cent of the electorate, Conservative candidates gained more than 48 per cent of the total vote (Pugh, 1992).

Despite the strong opposition to equal franchise among backbench Conservative MPs in the early 1920s, Conservative Party leaders realized that women voters were crucial to the party's electoral fortunes. According to *The Times*, there was an unusually heavy turnout of female voters in the December 1923 general election, and it was believed that the women's vote was a crucial factor in the Conservative Party's defeat (*The Times*, 7–8 December 1923). Sir George Younger, the Conservative Party chairman, agreed, claiming that women had voted against the party out of fear that its recently announced support for tariffs would make food more expensive (Pugh, 1992). Lady Astor also thought that the reduced support from women voters had been responsible, but she attributed this to the party's indifference to women's issues, such as equal franchise reform (*The Times*, 12 December 1923: 13). Astor's public criticism of her own party drew attention to its need to strengthen its appeal to women voters; it is not surprising, therefore, that the party made special efforts to attract them in the 1924 general election.

It has been suggested that the Conservative Party's commitment to expanding the female electorate emerged from its policy towards Adamson's 1924 suffrage bill. Although wanting Conservative MPs to vote against the bill, Conservative Party leaders did not wish to alienate existing female voters by opposing the equal franchise principle. Therefore, while conceding the desirability of equal franchise rights, they insisted that a conference on electoral reform be held first, which was intended to obtain all-party support for equalization of the franchise at age 25 (Close, 1977). This formulation failed to maintain party unity: while 72 Conservative MPs voted against the bill,

50 voted for it. But it was very likely the origin of Baldwin's statement on women's suffrage a few months later during the general election.

CONSERVATIVE PARTY REFORM PLEDGE

Although the 1924 Conservative Party election manifesto made greater efforts to appeal to women, it contained no reference to women's suffrage. But just before the election Stanley Baldwin, the party leader, declared that the Conservative Party supported equal political rights for women. He made no commitment as to how soon it might implement this pledge. He did, however, indicate that if the party was returned to office it would propose an all-party conference on franchise reform similar to the 1916 Speaker's Conference.

Suffrage advocates were uncertain as to how firmly Baldwin had committed a Conservative Government to reform. Those who were not Conservatives suspected that Baldwin's statement was intended to attract female voters while leaving a Conservative Government free to postpone action into the indefinite future. Some prominent Conservatives, including Winston Churchill, privately believed Baldwin had merely pledged support for the equal franchise principle without making any commitment to act beyond sponsoring a conference.

Baldwin's proposal to hold an all-party conference was politically shrewd. It enabled suffrage reformers to believe he was proceeding towards reform, while allowing opponents to view it as a means of blocking reform. In addition to holding his party together, Baldwin apparently also hoped that through it he could commit the Labour Party to an agreed measure granting equal franchise at age 25. This would have permitted him to fulfill his equal franchise pledge while gaining approval from anti-democratic Conservatives who wished to minimize the increase in the electorate. But if this was his plan, it collapsed when Labour refused to agree to setting the voting age at 25.

How the 1924 Conservative Government came to introduce equal franchise at age 21 has been a matter of controversy. The Cabinet faced three main issues: (1) Should it limit itself to proposing an all-party conference without any commitment to action if the conference was deadlocked? (2) Should it agree to introduce franchise legislation in the current Parliament? (3) If equal franchise was to be introduced, should it be granted at age 21 or 25?

Baldwin's ambiguous franchise reform declaration contributed to the conflicting views as to the government's policy. In pledging the party to equal political rights during the 1924 election campaign, Baldwin stated that the question should be settled, 'if possible', by agreement, and that an all-party conference be appointed to accomplish this. But this left unresolved the question of what the Conservative Government would do if it was not possible to settle the matter by agreement. The statement may have been deliberately vague because the party was so divided by the issue. Reformers interpreted Baldwin's statement as indicating a preference to proceed with reform via the method of an all-party conference, but implying a commitment to introduce equal franchise regardless of whether this method was used. Reform opponents interpreted it as supporting the equal franchise principle, but without any commitment to action other than sponsoring a conference which might be unable to reach agreement.

The Cabinet was forced to consider its position by the private member's equal franchise bill introduced in February 1925. The minutes indicate the Cabinet agreed that Sir William Joynson Hicks, the Home Secretary, was to announce the government's opposition to the bill. In doing so, he was to refer to the Prime Minister's 1924 election pledge, and to state that the government intended to give effect to it later in the present Parliament by proposing an all-party conference. When he addressed the House of Commons, Joynson Hicks stated that the government was committed to equal franchise before the next general election. The House then voted for a government amendment proposing that 'a considered scheme of franchise reform' should be introduced into the House 'within the lifetime of the present Parliament' (Butler, 1963).

Churchill later claimed that Joynson Hicks' statement had inadvertently pledged the government to introduce equal franchise before the end of the current Parliament without Cabinet authorization. But Baldwin, who surely knew what his pledge meant, was sitting next to Joynson Hicks when the latter spoke and made no objection. Furthermore, when Baldwin spoke later in the debate he did not repudiate Joynson Hicks' statement. Joynson Hicks responded to Churchill's claim by pointing out that the Cabinet had approved the amendment put to the House, and in doing so had agreed to franchise reform in the current Parliament, with or without a conference. Churchill's insistence that the Cabinet had only approved a scheme of franchise reform that emerged from an all-party conference may have reflected his hope that the latter would be deadlocked, thus preventing reform.

WOMEN'S REFORM STRATEGIES

By the mid-1920s the lack of visible progress towards reform had begun to produce tension between the women's societies. Rathbone, Rhondda, and Astor urged three alternative strategies to improve this situation. Under Rathbone's leadership the NUSEC continued its non-confrontational and non-partisan efforts to organize support from the three major parties. It sponsored public rallies for equal franchise – some 200 in 1927 alone – to demonstrate support for reform, but it placed special importance on the kind of backstage lobbying, much of it done by Eva Hubback, that remained largely unknown to the public (Pedersen, 2004). In addition to the individual meetings with MPs when suffrage bills were being considered, Rathbone and Hubback organized deputations to the major party organizations prior to each general election in an attempt to persuade them to include equal franchise rights in their platforms. Rathbone and Eva Hubback were also very skillful in getting letters to the editor published in *The Times* and other influential newspapers [**Doc. 33, p. 137**]. But since most of this work took place behind the scenes, it left some reform advocates with the impression that little had been accomplished.

Impatient with the NUSEC's lack of success, Lady Rhondda (a prewar suffragette) sought to invigorate the suffrage campaign by bringing Mrs Pankhurst into it and reviving the suffragette tactic of protest demonstrations. In 1926 Rhondda established the **Equal Political Rights Demonstration Committee** (EPRDC) as a step in this direction. Its original purpose was solely to organize the 3 July Hyde Park mass meeting which 40 women's groups supported. Nearly 3,000 women participated in the first suffrage procession since the First World War; the press portrayed it as a revival of the pre-war militant spirit.

Following the rally, the pre-war tensions between the movement's suffragist and suffragette wings revived. Lady Rhondda's paper, *Time and Tide*, criticized the NUSEC's previous efforts by claiming that the Hyde Park rally demonstrated that the women's movement had shaken off the sense of 'political lassitude' that had resulted from the movement's tendency to 'spread itself thin' in supporting too many reforms (Alberti, 1989: 186–7). This was apparently intended to justify replacing the suffragists (mainly from the NUSEC) by ex-suffragettes as the suffrage campaign's leaders. Although the EPRDC had been created solely to sponsor the July demonstration, shortly afterwards it was reorganized as the Equal Political Rights Campaign Committee with continuing responsibility for gingering up the suffrage campaign. Lady Rhondda, who was responsible for this action, chaired the new committee; its other officers, Ethel Froud and Rebecca West, were also ex-suffragettes. This threatened to revive the pre-war split between the suffragettes and suffragists. This step was supported by the societies that included pre-war militants – the Six Point Group, the WFL, St Joan's, and the National Union of Women Teachers – but those that were led by suffragists – the NUSEC, the LNSWS and the National Council of Women – opposed it (LNSWS Executive Committee minutes, 1926). The NUSEC leaders recognized that the change was an attempt to wrest control of the suffrage campaign out of their hands, and feared that Rhondda would resurrect militant

Equal Political Rights Demonstration Committee: An umbrella organization established in 1926 with Lady Rhondda as its leader. Dissatisfied with the lack of progress towards equal franchise, Rhondda believed more militant tactics were needed. After sponsoring a mass demonstration in July 1926, the committee changed its name to the Equal Political Rights Campaign Committee.

tactics that would prevent reform. Later, after Lady Rhondda promised that membership would not bind the NUSEC to any action of which it disapproved, the NUSEC agreed to join (NUSEC Executive Committee minutes, 1927).

While Rhondda wanted women to take a visible role in pressuring the government to grant equal suffrage so that they could be seen to have been responsible for reform, Rathbone and Lady Astor warned her against confrontational tactics. Astor was orchestrating pressure by Conservative women within the party structure, and was convinced that Baldwin would proceed with reform unless suffragette militancy revived (Harrison, 1983).

Uncertainty about the government's position contributed to tensions within the women's groups as to what they should demand. At the Consultative Committee's October 1926 meeting the societies disagreed over how they should respond if the government did set up a franchise conference. Eva Hubback, speaking for NUSEC, thought they should accept, but withdrew her suggestion when the WFL and St Joan's representatives objected on the ground that it was just a ploy to avoid introducing legislation (Consultative Committee minutes, 1926).

Feminists were also divided as to whether they should accept if the government proposed equal franchise at age 25 or hold out for age 21. Although the NUSEC was pledged to fight for age 21, in November 1925 it urged the Consultative Committee to accept age 25; this was opposed by the WFL and St Joan's representatives (Consultative Committee minutes, 1925). Lady Astor also urged the women's organizations to accept age 25 if the government offered it. Rathbone privately agreed on the necessity of compromise, but feared that Lady Rhondda would not accept it. If the government proposed suffrage at age 25 Rathbone planned to 'get on her [Rhondda] at once . . . and try to make her take the same line' (Alberti, 1989: 187).

Astor's efforts to mobilize Conservative Party women to pressure the government were hampered by the divisions within their ranks. The 1926 Conservative Party women's conference defeated a motion calling for equal franchise at age 21, but passed one urging that it be granted at age 25. When the party's Women's Advisory Committee discussed the issue on 16 November 1926 they found that Conservative women were divided between those who wished: (1) that women be given the vote at age 21; (2) that equal franchise be granted at age 25; and (3) that reform be limited to removing the anomalies in the current law so that all women aged 30 and above could vote. They were in agreement, however, that the government had made a promise to deal with the issue, and informed the Home Secretary that it would be 'disastrous' if it did not do so before the next election [**Doc. 34, p. 138**].

The opposition to equal franchise within the Conservative Party was so strong that when the Conservative Government was established in 1924, Eva Hubback believed that equal franchise was the least likely of the NUSEC reforms to be achieved (Alberti, 1989). Baldwin's determination to introduce equal franchise legislation was decisive during the crucial period in 1927 when the Cabinet reluctantly agreed to this. While the independent women's movement – especially the NUSEC – played a key role in keeping the issue alive in Parliament, Pedersen notes that it was not responsible for the Cabinet's decision to proceed with legislation (Pedersen, 2004). J. C. C. Davidson, the Conservative Party chairman, informed the Cabinet Equal Franchise Committee that the 'supporters of equal franchise were a very small if very vocal minority and commanded no general support' (Equal Franchise [Cabinet] Committee minutes, 21 February 1927). In the face of strong resistance within the Cabinet and minimal enthusiasm from the Conservative Party organization, Baldwin's commitment to reform appears to have been part of his strategy to make the Conservative Party the 'women's party' in order to offset the large number of working-class men enfranchised by the 1918 Reform Act who were expected to be Labour Party voters. The Conservative Party's success in attracting the women enfranchised by the 1918 Act encouraged the perception that it would benefit from the additional female voters (Jarvis, 1994).

On the day after receiving the Women's Advisory Committee's memorandum, the Cabinet created an equal franchise subcommittee to recommend how to implement the government's pledge concerning equal political rights for women. The subcommittee quickly ruled out an all-party conference, which would simply enable the Labour Party to champion votes for women at age 21. J. C. C. Davidson and the Conservative Central Office both warned the subcommittee that equal franchise at age 21 would be detrimental to party interests. Davidson claimed that it was politically impracticable to maintain the franchise age for women at age 30; he and the Central Office therefore recommended that equal franchise be granted at age 25 [**Doc. 35, p. 139**]. Perhaps because of the strong feeling developing within the subcommittee in support of this policy, Baldwin announced after three meetings that discussion would be continued in the Cabinet and the subcommittee was terminated.

Although a majority of the Cabinet initially resisted granting equal franchise rights at age 21, most were willing to concede it at age 25. But during the course of discussion the majority reluctantly accepted that the latter was politically impossible for at least two reasons. First, it meant raising the men's age from 21 to 25. This would antagonize young male voters and also give the party an undesirable anti-democratic image. Second, the party chairman and the Conservative Central Office were now recommending granting equal franchise at age 21 on the ground that if they didn't do it the next Labour Government certainly would, thereby obtaining the political loyalty of the new female voters. Therefore, Baldwin, Joynson Hicks, Lord Eustace Percy and Lord Robert Cecil insisted that the government proceed with equal political rights at age 21. Churchill and Lord Birkenhead (F. E. Smith) objected vehemently. Churchill felt so strongly that he insisted that his name be recorded as opposing the Cabinet's decision and attached a memorandum of dissent to the Cabinet conclusion. But even though the majority had little enthusiasm for equal franchise at age 21, they reluctantly accepted that setting it at age 25 was politically impractical, and on 12 April 1927 the Cabinet agreed to grant votes to women at age 21 [**Doc. 36, p. 139**].

Although this ended Cabinet discussion, opponents waged a last-ditch effort during 1927 to arouse Conservative Party opinion against equal franchise at age 21. Even after the Cabinet decision, in apparent violation of the principle of collective responsibility, Birkenhead continued to publish articles against age 21. The *Daily Mail* published a series of misleading articles claiming that the proposed reform meant giving the vote to 'flappers'. By portraying the latter as young, unmarried, independent, sexually active, and ignorant of politics the *Daily Mail* constructed a mixture of negative gender and generational stereotypes calculated to stir Conservative opinion against reform (Melman, 1988). The NUSEC leaders considered the press campaign an attempt to ignite a sex-war against women. They undercut this campaign by noting that 'responsible' people (notably Baldwin) frequently warned against class war, and asked: 'Is a sex war one jot less dangerous?' ('Waging the sex war', April 1927).

The most vehement equal franchise opponents portrayed it as a gender issue. Equal franchise legislation would make women a majority of the electorate, and some objected that men would be ruled by women. It was feared that women would vote as a gender bloc, bringing about the feminization of male political culture that many suffragists desired. Underlying the anti-equal franchise concern was an awareness that the younger women who would be enfranchised were more likely to be single, and therefore presumably more inclined to be feminist than older or married women [**Doc. 37, p. 140**]. The NUSEC's journal, the *Woman's Leader*, summed up the equal franchise resistance as based on 'sex prejudice, vague fears of petticoat government and the assumption that the five million women to be enfranchised are all cocktail drinking, Charleston dancing, flappers of 21 . . .' (*Woman's Leader*, April 1927).

While reform opponents portrayed it as part of a larger gender conflict in which women sought power at men's expense, reform advocates denied that it was a gender issue. Equal suffrage proponents argued that the political divisions among women were as great as those among men, and that the danger of women uniting to rule over men was illusory (Alberti, 1989: 185). Recognizing that the all-male House of Lords might vote against equal franchise if it was perceived as a gender issue, suffragists portrayed it as a representation issue. They noted that the women enfranchised under the 1918 Act were primarily married women, mostly homemakers, and that their interests were not identical to those of single women, many of whom were employed. This meant that when Parliament considered legislation affecting employed women, MPs did not have to be concerned about the views of the women whose interests would be affected. Feminists focused on this unfair denial of representation for employed women in letters to *The Times* and in their 8 March 1927 deputation to the Prime Minister [**Doc. 38, p. 140**].

The Conservative Party became reconciled to equal franchise legislation in the course of an intense intra-party debate during 1927. At the beginning of that year Conservatives were divided between those wanting no action other than holding an all-party conference and those desiring equal franchise at age 25. J. C. C. Davidson, the Conservative Party Chairman, informed the Cabinet Equal Franchise Committee on 21 February that the party's Central Office had not received a single resolution proposing equal franchise rights at age 21 (Equal Franchise [Cabinet] Committee minutes, 21 February 1927). A majority of the constituency associations that had expressed their view to the National Union executive by June 1927 favored equal franchise at age 25. By the end of 1927, however, the party had not only accepted equal franchise, but at age 21.

While the party's acceptance of the lower age could imply a conversion to the principle of gender equality, political expediency is a more plausible explanation. A majority of Central Office Agents had concluded by March that equal franchise at age 25 was impractical; it would antagonize large numbers of men while not satisfying the women who desired equal franchise at 21. Furthermore, they realized that the next Labour Government would almost certainly lower the voting age to 21 which would result in the newly enfranchised women becoming Labour voters. The NUSEC leaders considered the Conservative Party's dependence on their women's organization one of the most compelling reasons why it would eventually endorse equal franchise at age 21 ('Equal franchise', April 1927). Women on the National Union's Council had privately begun criticizing the government's failure to act as early as March 1927 (McCrillis, 1998). Their voices could not be ignored because by 1928 there were almost one million female Conservative Party members, far more than belonged to either of the other major parties. It was difficult for Conservative men to oppose equal franchise legislation without sounding anti-female, which was dangerous because by 1927 Conservative constituency organizations relied on their women members for fundraising, canvassing, and educational work (Close, 1977).

Although Conservative Party leaders had decided in favor of equal franchise at age 21, rank-and-file support for age 25 was so strong that party leaders needed adroit management to ensure that the party conferences

endorsed the lower age. Even the women's conference required careful handling. Eva Hubback, the NUSEC's Parliamentary Secretary, initiated the effort
to shift the 1927 Conservative women's conference towards equal franchise
at age 21. After noticing that the equal franchise resolution on the conference
agenda mentioned age 25, Hubback privately asked Marjorie Maxse, the
Conservative Central Office's chief organization officer, if the resolution
could be modified. Maxse contacted Lady Elveden, the Women's Unionist
Organization's Chair, who arranged for the reference to age 25 to be removed
and also asked several participants to make speeches in favor of age 21
(NUSEC Executive Committee minutes, May 1927). Also, in her address to
the conference, Lady Elveden defended equal franchise at age 21, insisting
that the majority of women under 25 who would be enfranchised would
become Conservatives ('Women Unionists and Franchise', 27 May 1927). Significantly, the women's conference applauded Baldwin when he admitted that
many of the women's local associations had 'strong feeling' for equal franchise
at 25. But he defended setting it at age 21 by noting that while it would make
women a majority of the electorate, this objection was pointless unless 'you
believe that the possession of the vote is the beginning of a sex war'. Since
his audience consisted of women who had explicitly rejected sex-war, Baldwin
thus shrewdly neutralized the women's resistance (*The Times*, 28 May 1927).

The struggle to secure party acceptance of equal franchise at age 21
culminated with the 1927 Conservative Party conference. Although three
resolutions were submitted opposing equal franchise at age 21, the conference endorsed the resolution favoring equal franchise at age 21 submitted by
a member of the party's Central Council.

When the Conservative Government introduced its 1928 equal franchise
bill, it was supported by the Liberal and Labour Parties; the opposition came
almost entirely from Conservative backbenchers. Although the Representation of the People (Equal Franchise) Bill passed its second reading in the
House of Commons in March 1928 by the overwhelming vote of 387 to 10,
this does not accurately reflect the size and intensity of the opposition. Aware
that many Conservative backbenchers would have opposed it if allowed a
free vote, the government applied the whips. Even so, an unusually large
number of Conservative MPs were absent when the division on the bill's second reading took place (although some claimed to have been absent because
they realized the vote would not be close, the absentees included a number
of prominent opponents, including Winston Churchill). The huge majority
also reflected prudence on the part of MPs who realized the bill was going to
pass, and that the female electorate could determine their political future.
Although a few Conservative diehards spoke against the bill during the
debate, the real struggle had already occurred before the measure reached
the House of Commons.

As a result of the Act women became a majority of the electorate, prising 52.7 per cent of the potential voters. The attacks on the 'flappe by equal franchise opponents obscured the fact that the Act enfran more women over 30 than under 25. Of the additional 5.5 million w who gained the vote, 1,950,000 were over age 30, while 1,590,000 were under age 25.

Although the 1928 Act was the culmination of a 61-year campaign for equal voting rights, reformers had mixed feelings. The NUSEC considered the Act the climax of a 'momentous' decade during which it had helped secure five major pieces of legislation benefiting women. But it warned that the women's gains had provoked a backlash involving restrictions on women's freedom to pursue paid employment that especially affected married women and women's opportunities for medical training (NUSEC, *Annual Report, 1928–1929*). Other feminists noted that there was still unfinished business: women were still excluded from the House of Lords and the diplomatic service, still often subjected to gender-differentiated pay scales and dismissed from their jobs when they married, and still treated as inferior in a variety of ways (Alberti, 1989). Reflecting on the anti-feminist reaction in the 1920s that, among other setbacks, had recently resulted in some London hospitals refusing to admit female medical students, Vera Brittain doubted that the struggle was really over. Since the suffrage campaign had originated amidst expectations that the vote would bring about a transformation of society, Brittain asked whether equal franchise meant women had 'really rounded seraglio point', or whether it had been granted because male politicians no longer feared women would vote as a bloc for gender reforms. If women were simply drawn into the existing parties and lacked the power to shape party programmes to protect their interests, Brittain anticipated that equal franchise would have little effect on existing gender structures (Gorham, 1996). If this should prove to be the case, equal franchise should be viewed as one stage of a continuing campaign to eliminate discrimination against women rather than a final victory.

Part 3

ASSESSMENT

8

Conclusion

The women's suffrage movement was a watershed in British women's history. It brought women together in a mass movement unparalleled in British history. It succeeded in gaining equal voting rights for women, the right of women to be elected to the House of Commons, and women's admission to the political parties. But for participants the sense of accomplishment was diluted by the awareness that the larger goal of undermining gender structures would be much more difficult to achieve than some had initially assumed.

Earlier studies viewed the suffrage campaign as narrowly concerned with equal political rights, and as a continuation of the movement towards political democracy associated with the Reform Acts of 1832, 1867, and 1884. It is now considered part of the gender reform movement initiated by Victorian feminists that was directed against women's subordinate roles in education, employment, and the family, as well as in politics. It was, in short, a movement for women's emancipation, not just for female enfranchisement.

The changed interpretation of the suffrage campaign in part stems from new understandings of its ideological basis. While some suffragists based their claim on an equal rights ideology rooted in liberal political theory, recent work has stressed the importance of a sexual difference ideology which maintained that women's natures were different from men's, and superior in important respects (Caine, 1992; Levine, 1987). This encouraged the perception that the vote would do more than simply allow women to vote as men did; it would empower women to alter man-made institutions to reflect women's higher moral standards. This was especially evident with respect to the double standard of sexuality, but it underlay a variety of other issues as well, including the use of force in domestic or international politics. Part of the male anti-suffragists' resistance to enfranchising females stemmed from the fear that women would use political power to feminize social institutions.

During the Edwardian period the suffrage campaign became a mass movement uniting women in a demand for gender reform fueled by a consciousness of oppression based on sex. But even during the peak period of gender consciousness reformers were divided by competing identities. Krista Cowman and Jill Liddington have explored the movement's class and regional dimensions (Cowman, *TCBH* 2002a, 2004; Liddington, 2006; Liddington and Norris, 1978), while Angela John and Leah Leneman have demonstrated the continued importance of ethnic identity (John, 1991; Leneman, 1991). Party ties also threatened to undermine gender unity; Claire Hirshfield has described the anguish of Liberal Party women forced to choose between gender and party loyalties (Hirshfield, 1990), while several authors have examined how Labour women dealt with this dilemma (Hannam and Hunt, 2001; Cowman, 2004; Collette, 1989). In the post-war decade party affiliation and ideological differences hampered efforts to re-establish a united women's movement (Pedersen, 2004; Smith in Smith, 1990).

The relative importance of the NUWSS and the WSPU in gaining the vote continues to be a matter of debate. There is general agreement that the WSPU's militant tactics revitalized the suffrage movement between 1905 and 1908 and drew many women into the campaign who had previously remained aloof (Cowman, 2004; Purvis, 2002; Liddington, 2006). The increased scrutiny of the WSPU branches in the regions has drawn attention to the importance of women on the left in the WSPU, even after the split with the Women's Freedom League (Cowman, 2004; *HWJ*, 2002b). But the new forms of violence used by the WSPU after 1912 impeded further progress towards franchise reform. Studies by Sandra Holton and Jo Vellacott have suggested that the NUWSS's electoral alliance with the Labour Party was the key development within the women's movement in bringing about women's suffrage (Holton, 1986, 1996; Vellacott, 1993).

Antoinette Burton has drawn attention to the danger of viewing the suffrage movement in isolation from the political and cultural context in which it developed. While suffragists sought to establish a 'global sisterhood' through such organizations as the International Women's Suffrage Alliance, they also collaborated in the ideological work of sustaining the British Empire (Burton, 1994). The tension between these positions was reflected in suffragists' arguments for enfranchisement. Some held that women's suffrage was desirable in order to replace a masculine political culture relying upon physical force by a female culture based upon moral principles. But others believed that women needed the vote in order to help Britain continue to be a great imperial nation. The First World War brought the conflict between the two positions into the open, resulting in the split in the NUWSS in 1915.

Did women's suffrage make a difference? In a variety of ways, it had immediate consequences. Women became members of the leading political parties, had a voice in party deliberations, and could become MPs. After partial enfranchisement in 1918, there was a surge of legislation that opened certain professions to women, improved women's guardianship rights over their children, provided state pensions for widowed mothers and orphans, increased the financial support that a father could be required to pay for an illegitimate child, and improved health and welfare facilities for women and children, among other reforms (Thane in Vickery, 2001). Also, as Jon Lawrence has noted, British politics became less violent during the inter-war period, and the need to cultivate women voters contributed to this (Lawrence in Vickery, 2001).

But it would be misleading to overstate the immediate impact of women's enfranchisement. The granting of equal suffrage rights was not accompanied by dramatic changes in gender structures or attitudes towards gender roles. Hannam and Hunt conclude that in many respects the gender division of labor in the workplace as well as in the home 'was reinforced rather than weakened' during the inter-war years (Hannam and Hunt, 2001: 128). The marriage bar, for example, was enforced more vigorously in teaching and the civil service after the war, gendered pay was more consistently imposed on female employees, and the Sex Disqualification (Removal) Act proved an ineffective weapon in obtaining equal opportunities for women even though it did remove certain legal barriers (Smith in Smith, 1990). While women could become MPs, in practice few were able to do so. Women who entered the major political parties during the inter-war period often found that they were expected to be canvassers and fundraisers, not policy-makers.

Some of the suffragists who had been prominent in the NUWSS/NUSEC suffrage campaigns continued to be leaders of the post-suffrage women's movement. Eleanor Rathbone and Ray (and Pippa) Strachey were key figures in the campaigns for family allowances and equal pay in the 1930s and 1940s. The enfranchisement of women made them a potentially powerful political force, especially in close elections. This was an important consideration in the decision to grant equal pay to female civil servants in the mid-1950s (Smith, 1992). The growing awareness of the difficulty of using political action to bring about gender reform has been a sobering discovery for many reformers, but change has occurred even if the pace has sometimes seemed glacial.

Part 4

DOCUMENTS

THE FIRST SUFFRAGE PETITION   **Document 1**

In the 1860s the idea of women voting seemed so radical that reformers thought it best to base their proposal on property ownership rather than sex discrimination.

It seems to me that while a Reform Bill is under discussion and petitions are being presented to Parliament from various classes . . . it is very desirable that women who wish for political enfranchisement should say so. . . . I think the most important thing is to make a demand and commence the first humble beginnings of an agitation for which reasons can be given that are in harmony with the political ideas of English people in general. No idea is so universally accepted and acceptable in England as that taxation and representation ought to go together, and people in general will be much more willing to listen to the assertion that single women and widows of property have been unjustly overlooked, and left out from the privileges to which their property entitles them, than to the much more startling general proposition that sex is not a proper ground of distinction in political rights.

It seems to me, therefore, that a petition asking for the admission to the franchise of all women holding the requisite property qualification would be highly desirable now. . . .

Source: Helen Taylor to Barbara Bodichon, 9 May, 1866. The Women's Library, McCrimmon Bodichon Collection.

SEXUAL DIFFERENCE AND WOMEN'S SUFFRAGE   **Document 2**

Although some reformers based their claim on liberal equal rights ideology, many insisted it was because women were different from men that they should have the right to vote.

With regard to the differences between men and women, those who advocate the enfranchisement of women have no wish to disregard them or make little of them. On the contrary, we base our claim to representation to a large extent on them. If men and women were exactly alike, the representation of men would represent us; but not being alike, that wherein we differ is unrepresented under the present system. . . .

But this difference between men and women, instead of being a reason against their enfranchisement, seems to me the strongest possible reason in favour of it; we want the home and the domestic side of things to count for more in politics and in the administration of public affairs than they do at present. We want to know how various kinds of legislative enactments bear on the home and on domestic life. And we want to force our legislators to consider the domestic as well as the political results of any legislation which many of them are advocating. . . .

I advocate the extension of the franchise to women because I wish to strengthen true womanliness in woman, and because I want to see the womanly and domestic side of things weigh more and count for more in all public concerns.

Source: Millicent Garrett Fawcett, 'Home and Politics', in J. Lewis (ed.), *Before the Vote Was Won: Arguments for and Against Women's Suffrage* (London: Routledge, 1987), pp. 419, 423.

Document 3   THE CASE FOR WOMEN'S SUFFRAGE

Anti-suffragists relied heavily on the idea of separate spheres, with its belief that political life is part of men's sphere because it is based on physical force.

You are generally told that women are not fit to vote . . . [but] women are held fit to possess property, and the possession of property is the only fitness for the vote. But if we press for particulars, we are met by the great Nature-argument; we are told of the peculiarities of our nature . . . that is, in other words, our physical and mental inferiority. . . .

There is one more argument that I must notice – that the basis of government is physical force . . . and therefore women being physically the weaker are unfitted for the franchise. . . . But what is meant by physical force being the basis of government? I have always thought that government was designed to supersede physical force, that civilization meant the reign of law instead of brute-strength. . . . Doubtless, before communities were formed, the man who could knock the other down would have most power. But . . . our Cabinet ministers are not chosen from the men who can knock each other down.

Source: Arabella Shore, speech delivered to the London National Society for Women's Suffrage in P. Hollis (ed.), *Women in Public 1850–1900* (London: Allen and Unwin, 1979), pp. 309, 311.

Document 4   WOMEN AGAINST WOMEN'S SUFFRAGE

Female anti-suffragists were convinced that women's suffrage would erode the difference between men's and women's natures by lowering women to the men's level.

We, the undersigned, wish to appeal to the common sense and the educated thought of the men and women of England against the proposed extension of the Parliamentary suffrage to women.

1. While desiring the fullest possible development of the powers, energies, and education of women, we believe that their work for the State, and their responsibilities towards it, must always differ essentially from those of men. . . . To men belong the struggle of debate and legislation in Parliament; the hard and exhausting labour implied in the administration of the national resources and powers; the conduct of England's relations towards the external world; the working of the army and navy. . . . In all these spheres women's direct participation is made impossible either by the disabilities of sex, or by strong formations of custom and habit resting ultimately upon physical difference, against which it is useless to contend. . . . Therefore, it is not just to give women direct power of deciding questions of Parliamentary policy, of war, of foreign or colonial affairs, of commerce and finance equal to that possessed by men. . . .

To sum up: we would give them [women] their full share . . . in that higher State which rests on thought, conscience, and moral influence; but we protest against their admission to direct power in that State which does rest upon force – the State in its administrative, military and financial aspects – where the physical capacity . . . of men ought to prevail. . . .

Source: 'An Appeal Against Female Suffrage', *The Nineteenth Century* (June 1889) in P. Hollis (ed.), *Women in Public 1850–1900* (London: Routledge, 1979), pp. 322–3.

FAWCETT'S RESPONSE TO FEMALE ANTI-SUFFRAGISTS   **Document 5**

Millicent Fawcett considered it illogical that voting should be considered a threat to women's femininity, but that working for male candidates in parliamentary elections was considered acceptable.

A large part of the Protest [against women's suffrage] is directed against women taking an active part in the turmoil of political life. . . . On the other hand, women do not vote in Parliamentary elections, but they are invited and pressed by all parties to take an active part in the turmoil of political life. Among other inconsistencies of the protesting ladies, it should not be forgotten that . . . if women are fit to advise, convince, and persuade voters how to vote, they are surely also fit to vote themselves. . . .

The 'party nothing but party' politician in England . . . looks with distrust on women's suffrage. Women would be an unknown quantity, less amenable to party discipline. . . . These fears tell against us very heavily, and we cannot allay them; because the fear that women will be independent and will dare to vote for what they think is right, whether the professional politician likes it or not, is, in our minds, not a fear, but a hope, and a hope which is at the root of all we are working for. . . .

We do not want women to be bad imitations of men; we neither deny nor minimise the differences between men and women. The claim of women to representation depends to a large extent on those differences.

Source: Millicent Garrett Fawcett, 'Female Suffrage: A Reply' *The Nineteenth Century* (July 1889) in P. Hollis (ed.), *Women in Public 1850–1900* (London: Routledge, 1979), pp. 330–31.

Document 6   BEATRICE WEBB ENDORSES WOMEN'S SUFFRAGE

In her letter to Millicent Fawcett, Beatrice Webb explains that it was not a belief in 'women's rights' that converted her to women's suffrage, but an awareness that Parliament was becoming increasingly involved with issues that were part of women's sphere, such as health, education, and welfare.

My objection [to women's suffrage] was based principally on my disbelief in the validity of any 'abstract rights', whether to votes or to property. . . .

I thought that women might well be content to leave the rough and tumble of party politics to their mankind, with the object of concentrating all their own energies on what seemed to me their peculiar social obligations. . . .

Such a division of labour between men and women is, however, only practicable if there is among both sections alike, a continuous feeling of consent to what is being done by government. . . . This consciousness of consent can hardly avoid being upset if the work of government comes actively to overlap the particular obligations of an excluded class. . . . The rearing of children, the advancement of learning, and the promotion of the spiritual life – which I regard as the particular obligations of women – are, it is clear, more and more becoming the main preoccupations of the community as a whole. The legislatures of this century are, in one country after another, increasingly devoting themselves to these subjects. Whilst I rejoice in much of this new development of politics, I think it adequately accounts for the increasing restiveness of women. They are, in my opinion, rapidly losing their consciousness of consent in the work of government and are even feeling a positive obligation to take part in directing this new activity. This is, in my view, not a claim to rights or an abandonment of women's particular obligations, but a desire more effectively to fulfill their functions by sharing the control of state action in those directions.

Source: Beatrice Webb to Mrs [Millicent] Fawcett, 5 November 1906 in Barbara Drake and Margaret Cole (eds), *Our Partnership* (Cambridge University Press, 1975), pp. 362–3.

FAWCETT AND WSPU MILITANCY   **Document 7**

Although reluctant to condemn WSPU militancy publicly, Millicent Fawcett believed that law and order were especially important to women and that this was being undermined by the WSPU's campaign.

I still feel disinclined to encourage one set of suffragists to denounce another set. Though I feel most strongly the essential immorality of issuing a call to the roughs of London to come and 'rush' the House of Commons. . . . I feel that law and order are essential to all that makes life worth living and that they are especially and peculiarly vital to women.

Source: Millicent Garrett Fawcett to Philippa Strachey, 12 October 1908. The Women's Library, Autograph Collection, vol. 1C.

FAWCETT'S CASE FOR WOMEN'S SUFFRAGE   **Document 8**

Anti-suffragists based their case on sexual difference, but Fawcett demonstrates that it could also be used to support women's suffrage.

[Anti-suffragists] . . . go on repeating their catchword that 'Men are men and women are women,' meaning thereby that the point of view, the experience of life, the sphere of activity of women differ in many important respects from those of men, without seeing that these very facts are among the strongest and most irrefutable of the reasons for urging that no representative system is complete or truly national which entirely leaves out the representation of women. 'Women,' they urge . . . 'have different duties, different capacities, the woman's being in the spheres of Home, Society, Education, Philanthropy.' One would think that the obvious conclusion from this must be that when Parliament is dealing with legislation which concerns the home, society, education, or philanthropy, it would be well if there were some constitutional means of enabling the influence and experience of the average women of the country to make themselves felt.

Source: Millicent Garrett Fawcett, 'Men Are Men and Women Are Women', *The Englishwoman*, 1 (February 1909), pp. 17–31.

FAWCETT ON SEX-WAR   **Document 9**

Anti-suffragists claimed that female suffrage advocates were stirring up a sex-war, but Fawcett rejected the idea.

I never believe in the possibility of a sex war. Nature has seen after that: as long as mothers have sons and fathers daughters there can never be a sex war. What draws men and women together is stronger than the brutality and tyranny drawing them apart.

Source: Millicent Garrett Fawcett to Lady Frances Balfour, 5 March 1910. The Women's Library, Autograph Collection, vol. 1H1.

Document 10   SUFFRAGE AND SEX REFORM

Although Christabel Pankhurst is better known for linking women's suffrage with the control of male sexuality, NUWSS members had already made this connection before she took up the idea.

It will be found that everywhere the demand for women's political enfranchisement is rooted in and springs from one main fact. In . . . so long as women . . . are not full citizens so long must the evil continue of the double standard of morality for men and women. . . .

The question of sex morality which lies deep at the root of the Women's Suffrage question is one that affects the lives of women infinitely more closely than the lives of men. As I have said, immorality is almost always accounted a sin of the worst description in a woman, while in a man it is a slight offence easily forgotten and forgiven. Now we Suffragists want to change that false view. We want to make everybody feel that it is equally wrong for both sexes to transgress the moral law. I say especially we Suffragists, because our desire to win direct political power is founded upon our belief that in that way only shall we become possessed of the power and the weapons necessary to fight this terrible evil. The Women's Movement is in fact a great Moral Movement.

Source: Lady Chance, *Women's Suffrage and Morality: An Address to Married Women* (NUWSS, 1912), pp. 6, 8–9.

Document 11   MILITANCY AND THE DOUBLE SHUFFLE

Teresa Billington-Greig was one of the WSPU's most important early members, but became disillusioned with the Pankhursts.

What I condemn in militant tactics is the . . . crooked course, the double shuffle between revolution and injured innocence, the playing for effects and not for results – in short, the exploitation of revolutionary forces and enthusiastic women for the purposes of advertisement. These are the things by which militancy has been degraded from revolution into political chicanery. . . .

The chorus of approval . . . [of early militant acts] brought out another weakness: it confirmed in us the pose of martyrdom of which we had been rather ashamed until then, and it strengthened that curious mental and moral duplicity which allowed us to engineer an outbreak and then lay the burden of its results upon the authorities. . . .

The feeling within the Union against this double shuffle, this game of quick change from the garments of the rebel to those of the innocent martyr, was swamped by the public approval and extenuation of our protests. . . . We were accepted into respectable circles not as rebels but as innocent victims, and as innocent victims we were led to pose.

Source: Teresa Billington-Greig, 'The Militant Suffrage Movement', in C. McPhee and A. FitzGerald (eds), *The Non-Violent Militant: Selected Writings of Teresa Billington-Greig* (London: Routledge, 1987), pp. 138, 164–5.

SUFFRAGE MILITANCY AND WOMEN'S LIBERATION

Document 12

The WSPU appealed to young women in part because it encouraged them to throw off the restrictions imposed by contemporary sex roles.

One sometimes hears people who took part in the suffrage campaign pitied. . . . But for me, and for many other young women like me, militant suffrage was the very salt of life. The knowledge of it had come like a draught of fresh air into our padded, stifled lives. It gave us release of energy, it gave us that sense of being of some use in the scheme of things. . . . It gave us hope of freedom and power and opportunity. It gave us scope at last, and it gave us what normal healthy youth craves – adventure and excitement.

Source: Margaret Haig, *This Was My World* (1933) in G. Norquay (ed.), *Voices and Votes: A Literary Anthology of the Women's Suffrage Campaign* (Manchester: Manchester University Press, 1995), pp. 256–7.

SUFFRAGE MILITANCY AND THE SLAVE SPIRIT

Document 13

While the NUWSS seemed narrowly concerned with women's suffrage, the WSPU encouraged a revolt against all restrictions, in personal as well as public life, that denied women freedom.

Christabel [Pankhurst] was inspired not by pity but by a deep, secret shame – shame that any woman should tamely accept the position accorded to her as something less than an adult human being – a position half way between the child and the citizen. Christabel cared less for the political vote itself than for the dignity of her sex, and she denounced the false dignity earned by submission and extolled the true dignity accorded by revolt. She never made any secret of the fact that to her the means were even more important than the end. Militancy to her meant the putting off of the slave spirit.

Source: Emmeline Pethick-Lawrence, *My Part in a Changing World* (1938) in G. Norquay (ed.), *Voices and Votes: A Literary Anthology of the Women's Suffrage Campaign* (Manchester: Manchester University Press, 1995), p. 63.

Document 14   VIOLENCE AT SUFFRAGE MEETINGS

WSPU speakers, such as Hannah Mitchell, were frequently in danger of violent attack from males and could not be certain that the police would protect them.

The mob played a sort of Rugby football with us. Seizing a woman they pushed her into the arms of another group who in their turn passed her on. An elderly reporter protected me at first, but he soon collapsed. This frightened some of them and they drew off, but two youths held on to my skirt so tightly that I feared it would either come off or I should be dragged to earth on my face. But . . . I turned suddenly, gave one a blow in the face which sent him reeling down the slope, and pushed the other after him. . . . At last a group of men fought their way to me and Adela, having to beat off our assailants with their bare fists in order to get us out of the Clough. The crowd followed yelling like savages. . . . Eventually, with a number of men escorting us, we managed to board a tramcar, the last of the hooligans speeding our departure with a fusillade of cabbages . . . from the nearby gardens.

Source: Hannah Mitchell, *The Hard Way Up* (London: Faber and Faber, 1968), pp. 150–1.

Document 15   THE IMPORTANCE OF THE VOTE

Emmeline Pankhurst explained that women needed the vote because their perspective was different to men's, and laws made solely by men were unfair to women.

. . . it is important that women should have the vote in order that in the government of the country the women's point of view should be put forward. It is important for women that in any legislation that affects women equally with men, those who make the laws should be responsible to women in order that they may be forced to consult women and learn women's views when they are contemplating the making or the altering of laws. . . .

First of all, let us take the marriage laws. They are made by men for women. . . . Many a married woman having given up her economic independence in order to marry, how is she compensated for that loss? What security does she get in that marriage for which she gave up economic independence? Take the case of a woman who has been earning a good income. She is told that she ought to give up her employment when she becomes a wife and mother. What does she get in return? All that a married man is obliged by law to do for his wife is to provide for her shelter of some kind, food of some kind, and clothing of some kind. It is left to his good pleasure to decide what the shelter shall be, what the food shall be, what the clothing shall be. It is left to him to decide what money shall be spent on the home, and how it shall be spent; the wife has no voice legally in deciding any of these things. She has no legal claim upon any definite portion of his income. If he . . . chooses almost to starve his wife, she has no remedy. What he thinks sufficient is what she has to be content with.

. . . Take what happens to the woman if her husband dies and leaves her a widow, sometimes with little children. If a man is so insensible to his duties as a husband and father when he makes his will, as to leave all his property away from his wife and children, the law allows him to do it. That will is a valid one. So you see that the married woman's position is not a very secure one. It depends entirely on her getting a good ticket in the lottery. If she has a good husband, well and good: if she has a bad one, she has to suffer, and she has no remedy. That is her position as a wife, and it is far from satisfactory.

Now let us look at her position if she has been very unfortunate in marriage, so unfortunate as to get a bad husband, an immoral husband, a vicious husband, a husband unfit to be the father of little children. We turn to the Divorce Court. How is she to get rid of such a man? If a man has got married to a bad wife, and he wants to get rid of her, he has but to prove against her one act of infidelity. But if a woman who is married to a vicious husband wants to get rid of him, not one act nor a thousand acts of infidelity entitle her to a divorce; she must prove either bigamy, desertion, or gross cruelty, in addition to immorality before she can get rid of that man.

. . . By English law no married woman exists as the mother of the child she brings into the world. In the eyes of the law she is not the parent of her child. The child, according to our marriage laws, has only one parent, who can decide the future of the child, who can decide where it shall live, how it shall live, how much shall be spent upon it, how it shall be educated, and what religion it shall profess. That parent is the father.

Source: Emmeline Pankhurst, *The Importance of the Vote* (Woman's Press, 1908). Reproduced from Cheryl Jorgensen-Earp (ed.), *Speeches and Trials of the Militant Suffragettes: the Women's Social and Political Union, 1903–1918* (Madison, NJ: Fairleigh Dickinson University Press, 1999), pp. 32–4.

Document 16   BLACK FRIDAY

The following is a selection from the memorandum that the Parliamentary Conciliation Committee for Woman Suffrage sent to the Home Office after Black Friday with a request for a public inquiry into the conduct of the police.

The facts which gradually came to our knowledge regarding the behaviour of the police towards members of the Women's Social and Political Union on November 18, 22, and 23 have induced us to collect the testimony of women who took part in these demonstrations, and of eye-witnesses. . . .

They [the police] were instructed . . . to refrain as far as possible from making arrests. The usual course would have been . . . to arrest them [the women] on a charge of obstruction. . . . The consequence [of non-arrest] was that for many hours they were engaged in an incessant struggle with the police. They were flung hither and thither amid moving traffic, and into the hands of a crowd permeated by plain clothes detectives, which was sometimes rough and indecent. . . .

We cannot resist the conclusion that the police as a whole were under the impression that their duty was not merely to frustrate the attempts of the women to reach the House [of Commons], but also to terrorize them in the process. They used in numerous instances excessive violence, which was at once deliberate and aggressive, and was intended to inflict injury and pain. . . . They frequently handled the women with gross indecency. . . .

[Participant:] 'For hours one was beaten about the body, thrown backwards and forwards from one [policeman] to another, until felt dazed from the horror of it. . . . Often seized by the coat collar, dragged out of the crowd, only to be pushed helplessly along in front of one's tormentor into a side street . . . where he beat one up and down the spine. . . .'

The intention of terrorizing and intimidating the women was carried by many of the police beyond violence. Twenty-nine [of the 135 statements submitted to the committee] complain of more or less aggravated acts of indecency [by the police].

[Participant:] 'Several times constables and plain clothes men who were in the crowd passed their arms around me from the back and clutched hold of my breasts in as public a manner as possible, and the men in the crowd followed their example. . . .'

Source: H. N. Brailsford, Secretary of the Parliamentary Conciliation Committee for Woman Suffrage, 'Treatment of the Women's Deputations By the Police' 18 February 1911. National Archives, HO 144/1106/200455.

THE JOY OF BATTLE   **Document 17**

In her Queen's Hall speech shortly after Black Friday Mrs Pankhurst claimed that active participation in the battle for enfranchisement strengthened women by eradicating the submissive attitude expected of them.

I want to say a word about the men who have come into this fight. We women have known what the little gallant band of men have been doing for a very long time past, and we have been more grateful to them than I think perhaps they have realized. . . .

. . . This afternoon, although seventy of our dear women are in prison . . . we are full of hope and full of courage; yes, and I may say we are also full of joy in the new chivalry which is growing up amongst men, and we are full of joy because of the growing courage of women. . . . There is one thing which . . . [men] have kept from us, and that has been the joy of battle. They tell us women cannot fight. They tell us that warfare and strife are things that women must be kept out of because coming into it would destroy all that is best in them, all that is noblest in womanhood. . . . We know – every woman who took part in that Battle of Downing Street on Tuesday will agree – that there is something very strengthening in this strife, something very ennobling, and I believe it is good for the race that women should feel the joy of battle as well as men. I believe that it is good for the race that we women are having to fight for our freedom. I believe that we shall have a nobler and a finer race than we ever had when courage was a monopoly of men and submission was the monopoly of women.

Source: 'Fighting Speeches at Queen's Hall', *Votes for Women*, 2 December 1910. Reproduced from Cheryl Jorgensen-Earp (ed.), *Speeches and Trials of the Militant Suffragettes: the Women's Social and Political Union, 1903–1918* (Madison, NJ: Fairleigh Dickinson University Press, 1999), pp. 129–30.

Document 18   FAWCETT ON WSPU MILITANCY

Fawcett grew increasingly frustrated with WSPU militant acts that under-mined the NUWSS's efforts to build support for suffrage legislation.

I do think these personal assaults perfectly abominable and above all extra-ordinarily silly. The P. M.'s [Prime Minister's] statement on the 22nd was not just exactly all we wanted but it was better than anything that had ever been offered us before and was at any rate good enough to make *The Times* say the next day that it had made W. S. [women's suffrage] a question definitely before the country at this election and that if there is a Liberal majority it will be a mandate to grant suffrage to women. And then these idiots go out smashing windows and bashing ministers' hats over their eyes.

Source: Millicent Garrett Fawcett to Lady Francis Balfour, 28 November 1910. The Women's Library, Autograph Collection, vol. 1H3.

Document 19   FORCED FEEDING

Mary Richardson, one of the suffragettes who was force-fed, described what it was like in her autobiography.

The following morning horror of forcible feeding was announced by the rumbling of the wheels of the trolley approaching my cell door. I sat down on the floor and pushed my arms under and round the hot-water pipe. I intended to resist to the utmost. As I sat and waited five wardresses came in. They succeeded in loosening my hands and arm from round the pipe; and, when they had done this, they tried to lay me flat on the floor. I struggled with them. By the time I was on my back we were all breathless and panting. To my horror, then, four of the wardresses, who were all hefty women, lay across my legs and body to keep me pinned to the floor. And now that the victim was trussed up and ready the doctors came in drag-ging the hated trolley at their heels. One knelt to grip my shoulders, another lifted aloft the funnel that was to receive the liquid, the third knelt by my head and took the long tube in his hand and, little by little, forced the stiff nozzle at the end of the tube up my left nostril. As the nozzle turned at the top of my nose to enter my gullet it seemed as if my left eye was being wrenched out of its socket. Then the food, a mixture of cocoa, bovril, medicines and a drug to keep one from vomiting when the tube was drawn out, was poured into the funnel and down into my aching, bruised, quiver-ing body. . . .

After ten weeks of forcible feeding I was released, little better than a breathing corpse.

Source: Mary R. Richardson, *Laugh a Defiance* (London: Weidenfeld and Nicolson, 1953), p. 84.

KILL ME OR GIVE ME MY FREEDOM **Document 20**

Although she was so weakened by repeated hunger strikes that her followers feared for her life, Mrs Pankhurst insisted she would rather die than remain voteless.

. . . You know there is something worse than apparent failure, and that is to allow yourself to desist from doing something which you are convinced in your conscience is right, and I know that women, once convinced that they are doing what is right, that their rebellion is just, will go on, no matter what the difficulties, no matter what the dangers, so long as there is a woman alive to hold up the flag of rebellion. I would rather be a rebel than a slave.

. . . There is anarchy in a country which professes to be under constitutional and representative government, and denies the benefits of the constitution to more than half its people.

The anarchy is there, and we are trying to end it, and these men . . . know perfectly well that we are breaking the laws because we have had no voice in making them; . . . because we are taxed without being represented.

. . . I mean to be a voter in the land that gave me birth or that they shall kill me, and my challenge to the Government is: Kill me or give me my freedom. . . .

Source: 'Kill Me, or Give Me My Freedom!' *The Suffragette*, 18 July 1913. Reproduced from Cheryl Jorgensen-Earp (ed.), *Speeches and Trials of the Militant Suffragettes: the Women's Social and Political Union, 1903–1918* (Madison, NJ: Fairleigh Dickinson University Press, 1999), pp. 314, 316.

I INCITE THIS MEETING TO REBELLION **Document 21**

In her 17 October 1912 Albert Hall speech, Mrs Pankhurst urged her followers to rebel against the Government by attacking property.

What do we mean when we say we are going to continue the militant agitation for Woman Suffrage? . . . There is something that Governments care for far more than they care for human life, and that is the security of property.

Property to them is far dearer and tenderer than is human life, and so it is through property we shall strike the enemy. I have no quarrel with property, ladies and gentlemen, and it is only as an instrument of warfare in this revolution of ours that we make attacks upon property. I think there are a great many people who own property who understand it very well, but if they would only understand it a little more quickly they would do what we want them to do. We want them to go to the Government and say, 'Examine the causes that lead to destruction of property. Remove the discontent, remove the sense of outrage. . .'.

We women Suffragists have a great mission, the greatest mission the world has ever known. It is to free half the human race. . . . You, women in this meeting, will you help us to do it? ('Yes!') Well, then, if you will, put aside all craven fear. Go and buy your hammer; be militant. Be militant in your own way. Those of you who can express your militancy by going to the House of Commons and refusing to leave without satisfaction . . . do so. Those of you who can express their militancy by facing party mobs at Cabinet Ministers' meetings . . . do so. Those of you who can express your militancy by joining us in anti-Government by-election policy – do so. Those of you who can break windows – (great applause) – those of you who can still further attack the sacred idol of property so as to make the Government realise that property is as greatly endangered by women as it was by the Chartists of old days – do so. And my last word is to the Government. I incite this meeting to rebellion.

Source: 'Emmeline Pankhurst at the Albert Hall', *The Suffragette*, 25 October 1912. Reproduced from Cheryl Jorgensen-Earp (ed.), *Speeches and Trials of the Militant Suffragettes: the Women's Social and Political Union, 1903–1918* (Madison, NJ: Fairleigh Dickinson University Press, 1999), pp. 279, 281–2.

Document 22   SEX AND SUFFRAGE

In the last years before the First World War, Christabel Pankhurst argued that women needed the vote to protect themselves against male sexual abuse.

The sexual diseases are the great causes of physical, mental, and moral degeneracy, and of race suicide. As they are very widespread (from 75 to 80 per cent. of men being infected by gonorrhoea, and a considerable percentage, difficult to ascertain precisely, being infected with syphilis), the problem is one of appalling magnitude.

To discuss an evil, and then to run away from it without suggesting how it may be cured, is not the way of the Suffragettes, and in the following pages will be found a proposed cure for the great evil in question. That cure, briefly stated, is Votes for Women and Chastity for men. . . .

Regulation of vice and enforced medical inspection of the White Slaves is equally futile, and gives a false appearance of security which is fatal. Chastity for men – or, in other words, their observance of the same moral standard as is observed by women – is therefore indispensable.

. . . The cause of sexual disease is the subjection of women. Therefore to destroy the one we must destroy the other. Viewed in the light of that fact, Mr. Asquith's opposition to votes for women is seen to be an over-whelming public danger. . . .

The demand for Votes for Women means a revolt against wrongs of many kinds – against social injustice and political mismanagement. . . . But more than all it is a revolt against the evil system under which women are regarded as sub-human and as the sex-slaves of men.

Source: Christabel Pankhurst, *The Great Scourge and How to End It* (1913) in J. Marcus (ed.), *Suffrage and the Pankhursts* (London: Routledge, 1987), pp. 188–9, 194, 234.

ASQUITH AND SUFFRAGE REFORM   **Document 23**

When he met with the ELF deputation in 1914, Prime Minister Asquith gave the following response to their demand for women's suffrage.

On one point I am in complete agreement with you. I have always said that if you are going to give the franchise to women, give it to them on the same terms as to men. Make it a democratic measure. It is no good paltering with it. If the discrimination of sex does not justify the giving of the vote to one sex and withholding it from the other it follows a fortiori that the discrimination of sex does not justify and cannot warrant giving to women a restricted form of franchise while you give to men an unrestricted form of franchise. If a change is to come, it must be democratic in its basis.

Source: *The Suffragette*, 26 June 1914, p. 178.

RATHBONE AND THE ELECTION FIGHTING FUND   **Document 24**

Eleanor Rathbone was one of the strongest opponents within the NUWSS of its alliance with the Labour Party and its Election Fighting Fund policy.

The proposed Anti-government policy of the N. U. [NUWSS] will, if adopted, start it definitely on a path of what may be called constitutional coercion, as opposed to its previous record of constitutional persuasion. A step in that direction has already been taken by the formation of the Election Fighting Fund. We shall thus be moving one step nearer to the militancy of the W.S.P.U. and the [Women's] Freedom League. . . .

Already the Anti-Government policy of the W.S.P.U. has done something to create an impression, which hitherto the N. U. has done its best to counteract, of antagonism between Women's Suffrage and Liberalism. In [the] future, if the new policy is adopted, all Suffrage Societies will combine to strengthen that impression. . . .

Apart from its effectiveness as an instrument of coercion, the new policy raises several difficult questions. First, we talk of shortening the present Government's term of office. But . . . the trend of by-elections makes it more probable that the Conservatives will come into power next Parliament. If they do . . . I think it is pretty clear what to expect. We know that a far smaller proportion of Unionists are suffragists than of Liberals. . . .

Source: Eleanor Rathbone, 'The Gentle Art of Making Enemies: A Criticism of the Proposed Policy of the National Union', n. d. (1913). The Women's Library, NUWSS Papers, 2/NUWSS/B1/3, box 302.

———◆———

Document 25   SUFFRAGISTS AND THE PEACE MOVEMENT

Lord Cecil's warning against any NUWSS association with the peace movement probably reinforced Fawcett's own views on this matter.

Permit me to express my great regret that you should have thought it right not only to take part in the 'peace' meeting last night but also to have allowed the organization of the National Union [NUWSS] to be used for its promotion. Actions of that kind will undoubtedly make it very difficult for the friends of Women's Suffrage in both the Unionist and Ministerial [Liberal] parties.

Even to me the action seems so unreasonable under the circumstances as to shake my belief in the fitness of Women to deal with the great Territorial questions and I can only console myself by the belief that in this matter the National Union do not represent the opinions of their fellow countrywomen.

Source: Lord Robert Cecil to Mrs Henry Fawcett, 5 August 1914. The Women's Library, Autograph Collection, vol. 1K.

———◆———

THE SPLIT IN THE NUWSS   **Document 26**

The 1915 split in the NUWSS was especially bitter because those who resigned believed the NUWSS was repudiating the pre-war conviction that women would fundamentally transform politics.

The real cleavage of opinion in the Union [NUWSS] lies between those who consider it essential to work for the vote simply as a political tool, and those who believe that the demand for the vote should be linked with the advocacy of the deeper principles which underlie it.

This cleavage of opinion was clearly shown at the Council meeting, when a . . . majority . . . passed a number of resolutions founded upon the belief that 'the Women's Suffrage movement is based on the principle that social relations should be governed not by physical force but by recognition of mutual rights.' They were, however, not prepared to give effect to this decision. . . .

Do we ask for the vote merely as a political tool, or do we wish the National Union to link it with the advocacy of the deeper principles, the consciousness of which has been the source of so much vigor and impassioned devotion to our workers? . . .

The [resigning members] . . . believe that the Union cannot survive as a living organisation with the driving power of ideals behind it unless, at this tremendous crisis, it recognises the great principles for which it stands, and continues to uphold the ideal of the supremacy of moral force in human affairs. To this belief the N. U. has indeed already testified in its declaration against [WSPU] militancy.

Source: Catherine Marshall *et al.*, 'Statement By Retiring Members and Others', *The Common Cause*, 4 June, 1915, pp. 121–2.

THE CONSULTATIVE COMMITTEE'S RECOMMENDATION   **Document 27**

In August 1916 the Consultative Committee of Women's Suffrage Societies urged Prime Minister Asquith to include women's suffrage in any franchise reform legislation, and claimed that mothers were even more deserving of the franchise than female munitions workers.

The injustice of such exclusion [of women] . . . will become more intolerable than ever after the war, when the problem of the readjustment of men's and women's labour has to be faced. It is impossible to ignore the fact that the entry of large numbers of women into skilled occupations hitherto closed to them, and the discovery by employers of the great value of their labours, may possibly produce an apparent clashing of interests between the sexes, and that in solution of the problems that will arise the aid of Parliament may be invoked. It is contrary to every principle of British justice, as well as of democratic government, that such an issue should be dealt with by a body upon which two or three parties to the dispute – employers and the men workers – are fully represented, but over which the women workers have no control.

. . . Upon this and other problems of reconstruction after the war, we claim the right of women to a direct influence upon Parliament.

If a new qualification is to be established based on services in the war, then the claim of women to share in such a qualification cannot be ignored. The services they have rendered to the country have been so amply acknowledged, both by the Ministers mainly responsible for the direct conduct of the war and by those responsible for the maintenance of the country's industry, that we need not labour this point. We cannot believe that the compliments that have been paid to women have been empty words.

But there is another body of women who deserve, we think, even better of the country than the munitions and industrial workers and field labourers, and they are the women who have given their husbands and sons ungrudgingly to its defence. . . .

Source: Consultative Committee of Constitutional Women's Suffrage Societies to the Prime Minister, 4 August 1916. Reprinted from Midge Mackenzie (ed.), *Shoulder to Shoulder* (New York: Alfred A. Knopf, 1975), pp. 322–3.

Document 28   THE SPEAKER'S CONFERENCE AND WOMEN'S SUFFRAGE

W. H. Dickinson, one of the main women's suffrage advocates in the Speaker's Conference, was very concerned that the suffrage societies might reject the Conference's proposals because they did not include equal franchise rights for women.

I hope that you will not let the W. S. [Women's Suffrage] Societies rush to the conclusion that our [Speaker's] conference has done nothing for the cause. I think that when the recommendations appear you will find that you have something very substantial . . . only please do all you can to induce women to see that it will be bad tactics to fall foul of the conference because it may not have done all that they expected. The whole matter will need the most careful handling so as to avoid the risk of the Government having an excuse for saying that as it is impossible to satisfy the advocates of W. S. they refrain from dealing with W. S. at all.

Source: W. H. Dickinson to Mrs Henry Fawcett, 19 January 1917. The Women's Library, Autograph Collection, vol. 1L.

THE ORIGIN OF THE AGE RESTRICTION FOR WOMEN VOTERS   **Document 29**

In a private meeting with the NUWSS's spokesmen in the Speaker's Conference, Millicent Fawcett agreed to the imposition of an age limit for female voters as part of a compromise proposal to be introduced at the Conference.

Sir John Simon and Mr. Dickinson both considered there was a good chance of the [Speaker's] Conference recommending Women's Suffrage. The difficulty and danger would arise when concrete proposals for Women's Suffrage came to be discussed. The two Members of Parliament thought there was little or no chance of Adult Suffrage being recommended by the Conference and that for the Adultists to press for it would risk the loss of even a general recommendation for Women's Suffrage in any form. . . . A good deal of talk took place about various ways of dealing with the excess of women over men. Finally I think there was a general agreement that raising the voting age for women was the least objectionable way of reducing the number of women.

Source: Millicent Garrett Fawcett, 'Memorandum on conversation at Sir John Simon's house', 15 December 1916 [included with NUWSS Executive Committee Minutes, 4 January, 1917]. The Women's Library, NUWSS Papers, 2/NUWSS/A1/9, box 84.

THE NUWSS REACTION TO THE SPEAKER'S CONFERENCE PROPOSALS   **Document 30**

Many suffrage reformers were dissatisfied with the Speaker's Conference proposals for women's suffrage because they excluded most female factory workers.

Miss [Eleanor] Rathbone thought that the [Speaker's Conference] recommendations were not at all satisfactory as such a Franchise would be of no use to the [female] factory worker. We had been pressing for the Franchise on account of the industrial dislocation to be expected after the War. This basis would only enfranchise the wives of Trade Unionists who would vote with the men. She thought we might have to yield to it, but it seemed like throwing over the [female] factory worker altogether.

Mrs. Strachey thought that the basis was thoroughly unsatisfactory, but that as it had been accepted by the Speaker's Conference there was a strong presumption that it would also be accepted by the House. . . . We stand a chance of really getting something . . . now, and opposition to it based on however good reasons might wreck the chance altogether.

Source: NUWSS Executive Committee minutes, 1 February 1917. The Women's Library, NUWSS Papers, 2/NUWSS/A1/9, box 84.

Document 31   THE SUFFRAGE SOCIETIES' DEPUTATION TO THE PRIME MINISTER

When the deputation from the women's suffrage societies met with the Prime Minister, Millicent Fawcett assured him they would accept the government's proposals rather than insisting on equal franchise rights, but other members of the deputation reminded him that female munitions workers would remain disenfranchised under the government's scheme.

[Millicent Fawcett] I think I may say . . . that we shall be very gratified if . . . the Prime Minister should see his way to improve, in a democratic direction, upon the recommendations of the Conference – but only so far as is consistent with the safety of the whole scheme. . . . We should greatly prefer an imperfect scheme that can pass, to the most perfect scheme in the world that could not pass.

[Mary Macarthur] Women munition workers have asked me to say on their behalf that they do not ask for the vote as a reward for [wartime] services rendered. . . . They ask it because they want to play their part in the great reconstruction work that is lying ahead of us all. We know . . . there is no class which will be more affected . . . by reconstruction proposals than the women who have come into industry . . . during this emergency. . . . We feel bound to point out to you that the proposals of the Speaker's Conference shut the door against the vast majority of women engaged on munition work. . . .

Source: 'Women's Suffrage Deputation March 29, 1917'. House of Lords Record Office, Lloyd George Papers, F/229/3.

Document 32   THE CASE FOR EQUAL FRANCHISE

Eva Hubback was the NUSEC's parliamentary secretary in the 1920s.

It has become increasingly clear, election after election, that the woman who was enfranchised [in 1918] was either the married woman . . . or the woman of property. . . . The . . . situation thus became clear: it was the woman occupied in industry and in the professions . . . who by the terms of the [1918] measure were shut out from its advantages. It has been estimated, indeed, that only about one in fifteen of the women wage-earners have the right to vote. The great majority of women in industry leave before they are thirty to get married, while those over thirty in many cases live either with their families, or in furnished rooms, big hostels, etc. It is a matter of common knowledge that comparatively few professional women . . . are the proud possessors of houses, or even of unfurnished rooms of their own. The importance of this becomes manifest if we remember that almost every year

Parliament is discussing legislation . . . dealing with the conditions of . . . women workers. . . . In certain cases the interests of women workers clash with those of men. . . . It certainly cannot be right that the labour of adult women should be controlled by a Parliament which is not responsible to those whose livelihood it is directing.

Source: Eva Hubback, 'The Case For Equal Franchise', *Fortnightly Review*, CXXIII (April 1928), p. 529.

NUSEC BACKSTAGE WIREPULLING **Document 33**

Eleanor Rathbone's April 1927 letter conveys the NUSEC leaders' intense backstage efforts to secure support for equal franchise legislation.

. . . the effort of getting out that printed circular and all the individual letters, and telephoning generally left little time for anything else. Just as I was composing a letter to *The Times* commenting on their leading article, Miss Strachey rang up to say that she was getting Mrs Fawcett to send a telegram to each Member of the Cabinet. So the brilliant idea struck me of getting her to sign the letter to *The Times*, which she obligingly did (Fawcett I mean). Of course the result of getting all these things done in other people's names is that we shall get no credit for it. But it seemed the surest way of getting them done and really more effective than our own signatures. I have had word passed to MacMillan and one or two others so that they at least may know that we have pulled the strings.

The Times leader was written in the Astors' house so that suggestion has not been wasted. Your letter was in the *Observer* under a pseudonym and the effect showed in the note admitting the pledge. Talked to [Marjorie] Maxse and [J. C. C.] Davidson's Political Secretary on the phone and sent them our reprint.

Dr Jane Walker told us she had had a letter from Major Hill (most confidential) saying he knew *for certain* that the Government had decided on votes at twenty-one without a conference and that we had better do nothing. We saw him, Lady Astor and [Sir John] Newman in the House yesterday after the Budget. Betty is going to the House today at four to see if there is any announcement. Newman has promised to ring us up the moment he hears anything decisive. Lady A [Astor]. is worried because we are pressing for twenty-one; I reassured her that it was only on the tactical point. I surmise that possibly the Government has switched round to twenty-five and is going to push that through, giving as their excuse that the Labour Party have refused the Conference, so that they are free to drop the idea of an agreed measure. The tremendous barrage in the Press in favour of twenty-five makes this probable. If it should have turned out to be true, what shall we do about it? My idea is not to protest at the age, but make it perfectly clear that the one thing which concerns us is equal rights and that provided we are satisfied that the Government means business about that, the age on its merits does not concern us. If that happens, send an immediate wire saying if you have any suggestions differing from this; or telephone if you have detailed suggestions. I should get on to Rhondda at once if that happened and try to make her take the same line.

Source: Eleanor Rathbone to Eva Hubback, 28 April [1927] in Diana Hopkinson, *Family Inheritance: A Life of Eva Hubback* (Staples Press, 1954), pp. 92–3.

Document 34   CONSERVATIVE WOMEN DEMAND FRANCHISE REFORM

Although the Conservative Party's women's organization was divided over what reform should be introduced, they insisted that action by the government was necessary.

There is undoubtedly a growing feeling [among Conservative Party women] that if the Government do not see their way to appointing the Conference [on franchise reform], or to appointing it in such time as will allow of its finding becoming operative at the next Election, it will do us a lot of harm when that time comes.

There is no question of the merits of the case being involved and the opinion of Unionist women differs widely on the subject, but even among those who differ there seems to be a great measure of agreement that a promise has been made that the subject shall be dealt with, and that it will be very disastrous if the Prime Minister can be represented at the Election as not having redeemed a Pledge.

We [Conservative Party] depend at Elections upon masses of women with few really definite convictions, whose instincts are in the main naturally conservative but who might easily be swept away if their faith in the sanctity of the Prime Minister's pledges were shaken by skilful manoeuvres on the part of the enemy.

Source: Gwendolen, Lady Elveden to Colonel [F. S.] Jackson [Conservative Party Chairman], 16 November 1926. National Archives, HO 45/13020.

CONSERVATIVE PARTY OFFICIALS ON EQUAL FRANCHISE   **Document 35**

Although willing, with some reluctance, to accept equal franchise at age 25, the Conservative Party's Central Office warned that lowering it to 21 would significantly damage the party's electoral prospects.

It must I suppose be accepted as certain that the Government are committed to the introduction of a Bill to equalise the franchise for men and women. If this is not so, and there is still room for argument on the political question, we are decidedly of the opinion that the reduction of the franchise age in the case of women to 21 would have a detrimental effect on the fortunes of the Party. In . . . the industrial areas, particularly in those districts where women work in the mills, it is believed that such a measure would bring on to the electoral rolls a large majority of votes for the Labour Party, by reason of their being under the influence of the Trade Union officials.

We [Conservative Party Central Office] believe that if the age of franchise for women was reduced to 25, it would be politically better for the Conservative Party than 21, as particularly in the North of England, a large proportion of the women of 25 would be married and, therefore, much less likely to be led astray by extravagant theories.

Source: Conservative Party Central Office memorandum presented to the Cabinet Equal Franchise Committee on 21 February 1927. National Archives, CAB 27/336.

THE CABINET ADOPTS EQUAL FRANCHISE LEGISLATION   **Document 36**

Although the Cabinet preferred to grant equal franchise at age 25, it reluctantly accepted Baldwin's view that women's voting age be lowered to 21.

At the Cabinet Stanley [Baldwin] opened with a short résumé of the position with regard to our pledges on the women's vote concluding that the only thing we could do was to give it all round at 21. Winston [Churchill] led the opposition with great vehemence and our opinions were then taken all the way round. I took the view with many others that 25 for both sexes would be preferable but did not think we should see it through and therefore favoured 21 and without a conference beforehand. I did not think that we should lose particularly from the party point of view. . . . In the end 21 without a conference prevailed by a considerable majority. Winston very unhappy as indeed were also F. E. [Smith, Lord Birkenhead] and several others.

Source: Leo Amery diary, 12 April 1927 in J. Barnes and D. Nicholson (eds), *The Leo Amery Diaries, vol. 1: 1896–1929* (London: Hutchinson, 1980), p. 491.

Document 37 THE CASE AGAINST EQUAL FRANCHISE

Even after Baldwin announced the government's intention to introduce equal franchise legislation, some Conservatives continued to oppose the reform, warning that it would enfranchise young women who were likely to be feminists.

It cannot be said that this announcement [by Baldwin of an equal franchise bill] was received with enthusiasm, either by the supporters of the Government in the House, or by the Conservative Party, as a whole, in the country. Despite the strenuous and skilful propaganda issued by the Conservative central office, the Government's proposals received only very lukewarm support at the Cardiff [Conservative Party] Conference of 1927.

One effect, and that the most important effect, of the measure is that it will place for all time the women voters in a majority, not only in the country as a whole, but in practically every constituency. . . .

So far, it is true, there have been no signs of the formation of a feminist party, but one result of this Bill will be to increase enormously the number of unmarried women on the [election] register, and a small, but determined, feminist group, interested solely in feminist questions, might easily dominate the situation in those constituencies where the cleavage on normal political lines is into parties of approximately equal strength. The increase in the number of unmarried women voters will probably facilitate the formation of such groups.

Source: 'Backbencher', 'The Franchise Bill', *The English Review*, 46 (April 1928), pp. 394–5.

Document 38 THE SUFFRAGE SOCIETIES' DEPUTATION TO THE PRIME MINISTER

When the deputation from the suffrage organizations met with the Prime Minister, they did not base their case for equal franchise on the idea that women were entitled to equal rights, but claimed that employed women constituted an important economic group that was unable to use the ballot to defend its economic interests.

[Eleanor Rathbone] I desire only to make a single point. The great majority of women who work for their living, in industries or professions, are among the disenfranchised. Every year Parliament considers Bills, such as your own Factories Bill . . . which vitally affect the conditions under which those women earn their livings. . . . Whatever the merits of this legislation, it is dangerous that the women it concerns should be without the means of influencing Parliament which male workers possess. There is rivalry between men and women workers in many occupations. It cannot be said that in this matter the already enfranchised women adequately represent the unenfranchised. The majority of the enfranchised are wives and mothers, who may look at these questions of sex competition from the point of view of their husbands and sons, rather than of their unenfranchised sisters.

Source: 'Notes of Deputation from the Equal Political Rights Campaign Committee', 14 March 1927. National Archives, CAB 24/185/90.

———◄●►———

Guide to further reading

The place of publication is London unless noted otherwise.

There is an enormous and growing literature on the British women's suffrage campaign. The following is intended as a guide to some of the books that were most useful in preparing this volume, especially those that have appeared since the first edition (there is a more detailed bibliography of older material in the first edition of this book). Due to space limitations, I have not attempted to list journal articles, but would encourage the reader to consult the *Women's History Review*. The first edition of this book provides a list of memoirs and autobiographies by the participants in the campaign that should be useful to the student planning a research project.

Printed Primary Sources: There are several collections that are available including: J. Lewis (ed.) (1987) *Before the Vote Was Won: Arguments for and Against Women's Suffrage*, London: Routledge; J. Marcus (ed.) (1987) *Suffrage and the Pankhursts*, London: Routledge; C. McPhee and A. FitzGerald (eds) (1987) *The Non-Violent Militant: Selected Writings of Teresa Billington-Greig*, London: Routledge; and C. Jorgensen-Earp (ed.) (1999) *Speeches and Trials of the Militant Suffragettes: The Women's Social and Political Union, 1903–1918*, Madison, NJ: Fairleigh Dickinson University Press; and L. Delap, M. Dicenzo and L. Ryan (eds) (2006) *Feminism and the Periodical Press, 1900–1918*, Abingdon, Oxon: Routledge.

General Overviews: The student seeking an overview of the subject should find Sandra Holton's two books helpful: (1996) *Suffrage Days: Stories from the Women's Suffrage Movement*, London: Routledge; and (1986) *Feminism and Democracy: Women's Suffrage and Reform Politics in Britain 1900–1918*, Cambridge: Cambridge University Press. Also useful are S. Kent (1987) *Sex and Suffrage in Britain, 1860–1914*, Princeton, NJ: Princeton University Press; and M. Pugh (2000) *The March of the Women: A Revisionist Analysis of the Campaign for Women's Suffrage, 1866–1914*, Oxford: Oxford University Press.

On the relationship between feminist and suffrage ideas see L. Delap (2007) *The Feminist Avant-Garde: Transatlantic Encounters of the Early Twentieth Century*, Cambridge: Cambridge University Press.

Collected Essays: Some of the most important scholarship on the women's suffrage campaign has appeared in edited volumes. These include: J. Purvis and S. Holton (eds) (2000) *Votes for Women*, London: Routledge; C. Eustance, J. Ryan and L. Ugolini (eds) (2000) *A Suffrage Reader*, London: Leicester University Press; M. Joannou and J. Purvis (eds) (1998) *The Women's Suffrage Movement: New Feminist Perspectives*, Manchester: Manchester University Press; A. John and C. Eustance (eds) (1997) *The Men's Share? Masculinities, Male Support and Women's Suffrage in Britain, 1890–1920*, London: Routledge; J. Rendall (ed.) (1987) *Equal or Different: Women's Politics 1800–1914*, Oxford: Basil Blackwell; A. Vickery (ed.) (2001) *Women, Privilege, and Power: British Politics, 1750 to the Present*, Stanford, CA: Stanford University Press; H. L. Smith (ed.) (1990) *British Feminism in the Twentieth Century*, Aldershot: Edward Elgar; and M. Boussahba-Bravard (ed.) (2007) *Suffrage Outside Suffragism: Women's Vote in Britain, 1880–1914*, New York: Palgrave Macmillan.

The Victorian Suffrage Campaign: Those new to the subject might begin with P. Levine (1987) *Victorian Feminism 1850–1900*, London: Hutchinson. Also helpful are: S. Herstein (1985) *A Mid-Victorian Feminist: Barbara Leigh Smith Bodichon*, New Haven, CT: Yale University Press; J. Liddington and J. Norris (2000) *One Hand Tied Behind Us: The Rise of the Women's Suffrage Movement*, London: Rivers Oram Press; M. Shanley (1989) *Feminism, Marriage, and the Law in Victorian England*, Princeton, NJ: Princeton University Press; D. Rubinstein (1986) *Before the Suffragettes: Women's Emancipation in the 1890s*, Brighton: Harvester Wheatsheaf; June Hannam and Karen Hunt (2002) *Socialist Women: Britain, 1880s to 1920s*, London: Routledge; and B. Caine (1992) *Victorian Feminists*, Oxford: Oxford University Press.

The Constitutional Suffrage Societies: On the constitutional societies see: L. Hume (1982) *The National Union of Women's Suffrage Societies 1897–1914*, New York: Garland; D. Rubinstein (1991) *A Different World For Women: The Life of Millicent Garrett Fawcett*, New York and London: Harvester Wheatsheaf; L. Leneman (1991) *A Guid Cause: The Women's Suffrage Movement in Scotland*, Aberdeen: Aberdeen University Press; L. Tickner (1988) *The Spectacle of Women: Imagery of the Suffrage Campaign 1907–14*, London: Chatto and Windus B. Harrison (1978) *Separate Spheres: The Opposition to Women's Suffrage in Britain*, Croom Helm; M. Auchterlonie (2007) *Conservative Suffragists: The Women's Vote and the Tory Party*, London: I. B. Tauris; and J. Bush (2007) *Women Against the Vote: Female Anti-Suffragism in Britain*, Oxford: Oxford University Press.

The Militant Suffrage Societies: There are a number of valuable studies of the militant campaign: J. Purvis (2002) *Emmeline Pankhurst: A Biography*, London: Routledge; J. Liddington (2006) *Rebel Girls: Their Fight for the Vote*, London: Virago; K. Cowman (2004) *Mrs. Brown is a Man and a Brother!: Women in Merseyside's Organisations, 1890–1920*, Liverpool: Liverpool University Press; L. Mayhall (2003) *The Militant Suffrage Movement: Citizenship and Resistance in Britain, 1860–1930*, New York: Oxford University Press; M. Pugh (2001) *The Pankhursts*, London: Penguin; A. Rosen (1974) *Rise Up, Women! The Militant Campaign of the Women's Social and Political Union 1903–1914*, London: Routledge; B. Winslow (1996) *Sylvia Pankhurst*, London: UCL Press; P. Romero (1987) *E. Sylvia Pankhurst: Portrait of a Radical*, New Haven, CT: Yale University Press; L. Stanley and A. Morely (1988) *The Life and Death of Emily Wilding Davison*, London: The Women's Press; P. Bartley (2002) *Emmeline Pankhurst*, London: Routledge; V. Coleman (1996) *Adela Pankhurst: the Wayward Suffragette*, Melbourne: Melbourne University Press; and K. Cowman (2007) *Women of the Right Spirit: Paid Organisers of the Women's Social and Political Union 1904–18*, Manchester: Manchester University Press.

The NUWSS–Labour Alliance: In addition to the books by Holton, Hume and Pedersen mentioned elsewhere, the essential work on this topic is: J. Vellacott (1993) *From Liberal to Labour with Women's Suffrage: The Story of Catherine Marshall*, Montreal: McGill-Queen's Press.

The First World War and Suffrage: On suffrage during the war see the following: N. Gullace (2002) *'The Blood of Our Sons': Men, Women, and the Renegotiation of British Citizenship During the Great War*, New York: Palgrave Macmillan; S. Grayzel (1999) *Women's Identities at War: Gender, Motherhood, and Politics in Britain and France During the First World War*, Chapel Hill, NC: University of North Carolina Press; S. Kent (1993) *Making Peace: The Reconstruction of Gender in Interwar Britain*, Princeton, NJ: Princeton University Press; A. Wiltsher (1985) *Most Dangerous Women: Feminist Peace Campaigners of the Great War*, London: Pandora; M. Pugh (1978) *Electoral Reform in War and Peace 1906–18*, London: Routledge; and J. Vellacott (2007) *Pacifists, Patriots, and the Vote: The Erosion of Democratic Suffragism in Britain during the First World War*, New York: Palgrave Macmillan.

The Equal Franchise Campaign: The following are especially helpful on the 1920s: J. Alberti (1989) *Beyond Suffrage: Feminists in War and Peace, 1914–28*, Basingstoke: Macmillan; C. Law (1997) *Suffrage and Power: The Women's Movement 1918–1928*, London I. B. Tauris; M. Pugh (1992) *Women and the Women's Movement in Britain 1914–1959*, Basingstoke: Macmillan; B. Harrison (1987) *Prudent Revolutionaries: Portraits of British Feminists Between the Wars*,

Oxford: Oxford University Press; and S. Pedersen (2004) *Eleanor Rathbone and the Politics of Conscience*, New Haven, CT: Yale University Press.

Reference: Elizabeth Crawford has authored two essential reference works: (2005) *The Women's Suffrage Movement in Britain and Ireland: A Regional Survey*, Abingdon, Oxon: Routledge; and (1999) *The Women's Suffrage Movement: A Reference Guide*, London: UCL Press.

Archival Sources: There are two useful guides to archival sources: M. Barrow (1981) *Women 1870–1928: A Select Guide to Printed and Archival Sources in the United Kingdom*, London: Mansell; and H. Smith (1991) 'British women's history: the Fawcett Library's archival collections', *Twentieth Century British History*, 2: 2, pp. 215–23. The most important archival collections relating to the suffrage campaign are available at the Women's Library (formerly the Fawcett Library) in London. Adam Matthew has published several collections on microfilm: *Women, Suffrage and Politics: The Papers of Sylvia Pankhurst, 1882–1960*; *The Women's Suffrage Collection from Manchester Central Library*; *Women, Politics and Welfare: The Papers of Nancy Astor, 1879–1964*; and *Women's Suffrage and Government Control, 1906–1922*. On the militants see *Women's Social and Political Emancipation: The Suffragette Fellowship Collection in the Museum of London*, Harvester Press (mfm).

References

Place of publication is London unless noted otherwise.

Alberti, J. (1989) *Beyond Suffrage: Feminists in War and Peace, 1914–28*. Macmillan.

Bartley, P. (2002) *Emmeline Pankhurst*. Routledge.

Bearman, C. (2005) 'An examination of suffragette violence', *English Historical Review*, 120, pp. 365–97.

Burton, A. (1994) *Burdens of History: British Feminists, Indian Women, and Imperial Culture, 1865–1915*. Chapel Hill: University of North Carolina Press.

Butler, D. (1963) *The Electoral System in Britain Since 1918*. Oxford: Oxford University Press.

Caine, B. (1992) *Victorian Feminists*. Oxford: Oxford University Press.

Caine, B. (2005) *Bombay to Bloomsbury: A Biography of the Strachey Family*. Oxford: Oxford University Press.

Close, D. (1977) 'The collapse of resistance to democracy: Conservatives, adult suffrage and second chamber reform, 1911–1928', *Historical Journal*, 20, pp. 893–918.

Collette, C. (1989) *For Labour and for Women: The Women's Labour League, 1906–1918*. Manchester: Manchester University Press.

Consultative Committee of Women's Organisations minutes, 23 October 1924; 19 November 1925; 28 October 1926 in *The Records of the Women's Joint Congressional Committee*. Library of Congress (microfilm).

Cowman, K. (1998) ' "A party between revolution and peaceful persuasion": a fresh look at the United Suffragists', in M. Joannou and J. Purvis (eds), *The Women's Suffrage Movement: New Feminist Perspectives*. Manchester: Manchester University Press.

Cowman, K. (2002a) ' "Minutes of the last meeting passed": the Huddersfield Women's Social and Political Union minute book January 1907–1909, a new source for suffrage history', *Twentieth Century British History*, 13, pp. 298–315.

Cowman, K. (2002b) ' "Incipient Toryism"? The Women's Social and Political Union and the Independent Labour Party, 1903–14', *History Workshop Journal*, 53, pp. 129–48.

Cowman, K. (2004) *Mrs. Brown is a Man and a Brother!: Women in Merseyside's Organisations, 1890–1920*. Liverpool: Liverpool University Press.

Crawford, E. (1999) *The Women's Suffrage Movement: A Reference Guide 1866–1928*. UCL Press.

Crawford, E. (2005a) 'Police, prisons and prisoners: the view from the Home Office', *Women's History Review*, 14, pp. 487–505.

Crawford, E. (2005b) *The Women's Suffrage Movement in Britain and Ireland: A Regional Survey*. Routledge.

de Vries, J. (1994) 'Gendering patriotism: Emmeline and Christabel Pankhurst and World War One', in S. Oldfield (ed.), *This Working-Day World: Women's Lives and Culture(s) in Britain 1914–1945*. Taylor and Francis.

de Vries, J. (1998) 'Transforming the pulpit: preaching and prophecy in the British women's suffrage movement', in B. Kienzle and P. Walker (eds), *Women Preachers and Prophets Through Two Millennia of Christianity*. Berkeley: University of California Press.

'Equal franchise' *Woman's Leader*, 1 April 1927, p. 71.

Equal Franchise Committee minutes, 21 February 1927. PRO, CAB 27/336 E. F. (26) 3.

Frances, H. (1998) ' "Pay the piper, call the tune!": the Women's Tax Resistance League', in M. Joannou and J. Purvis (eds), *The Women's Suffrage Movement: New Feminist Perspectives*. Manchester: Manchester University Press.

Garner, L. (1984) *Stepping Stones to Women's Liberty: Feminist Ideas in the Women's Suffrage Movement 1900–1918*. Heinemann.

Gorham, D. (1996) *Vera Brittain*. Oxford: Blackwell.

Grayzel, S. (1999) *Women's Identities at War: Gender, Motherhood and Politics in Britain and France During the First World War*. Chapel Hill: University of North Carolina Press.

Gullace, N. (2002) *'The Blood of Our Sons': Men, Women and the Renegotiation of British Citizenship During the Great War*. New York: Palgrave Macmillan.

Hannam, J. (2000) '"I had not been to London": women's suffrage – a view from the regions', in J. Purvis and S. Holton (eds), *Votes for Women*. Routledge.

Hannam, J. and Hunt, K. (2001) *Socialist Women: Britain, 1880s to 1920s*. Routledge.

Harrison, B. (1978) *Separate Spheres: The Opposition to Women's Suffrage in Britain*. Croom Helm.

Harrison, B. (1983) 'Women's suffrage at Westminster 1866–1928', in M. Bentley and J. Stevenson (eds), *High and Low Politics in Modern Britain*. Oxford: Oxford University Press.

Harrison, B. (1987) *Prudent Revolutionaries: Portraits of British Feminists Between the Wars*. Oxford: Oxford University Press.

Heeney, B. (1988) *The Women's Movement in the Church of England 1850–1930*. Oxford: Clarendon Press.

Herstein, S. (1985) *A Mid-Victorian Feminist, Barbara Leigh Smith Bodichon*. New Haven, CT: Yale University Press.

Hirshfield, C. (1990) 'Fractured faith: Liberal Party women and the suffrage issue in Britain, 1892–1914', *Gender and History*, 2, pp. 173–97.

Hollis, P. (1987) *Ladies Elect: Women in English Local Government 1865–1914*. Oxford: Clarendon Press.

Holton, S. (1986) *Feminism and Democracy: Women's Suffrage and Reform Politics in Britain 1900–1918*. Cambridge: Cambridge University Press.

Holton, S. (1990) '"In Sorrowful Wrath": Suffrage Militancy and the Romantic Feminism of Emmeline Pankhurst', in H. L. Smith (ed.), *British Feminism in the Twentieth Century*. Aldershot: Edward Elgar.

Holton, S. (1996) *Suffrage Days: Stories from the Women's Suffrage Movement*. Routledge.

Holton, S. (2000) 'The making of suffrage history', in J. Purvis and S. Holton (eds), *Votes for Women*. Routledge.

Hume, L. (1982) *The National Union of Women's Suffrage Societies 1897–1914*. New York: Garland.

Hunt, K. (2000) 'Journeying through suffrage: the politics of Dora Montefiore', in C. Eustance, J. Ryan and L. Ugolini (eds), *A Suffrage Reader: Charting Directions in British Suffrage History*. Leicester University Press.

Jarvis, D. (1994) 'Mrs. Maggs and Betty: the Conservative appeal to women voters in the 1920s', *Twentieth Century British History*, 5, pp. 129–52.

Jarvis, D. (1996) 'British conservatism and class politics in the 1920s', *English Historical Review*, 111, pp. 59–84.

John, A. (ed.) (1991) *Our Mothers' Land: Chapters in Welsh Women's History, 1830–1939*. Cardiff: University of Wales Press.

John, A. (1995) *Elizabeth Robins: Staging a Life 1862–1952*. Routledge.

John, A. and Eustance, C. (eds) (1997) *The Men's Share? Masculinities, Male Support and Women's Suffrage in Britain, 1890–1920*. Routledge.

Kent, S. (1987) *Sex and Suffrage in Britain, 1860–1914*. Princeton, NJ: Princeton University Press.

Kent, S. (1993) *Making Peace: The Reconstruction of Gender in Interwar Britain*. Princeton, NJ: Princeton University Press.

Law, C. (1997) *Suffrage and Power: The Women's Movement 1918–1928*. I. B. Tauris.

Lawrence, J. (2001) 'Contesting the male polity: the suffragettes and the politics of disruption in Edwardian Britain', in A. Vickery (ed.), *Women, Privilege, and Power: British Politics, 1750 to the Present*. Stanford, CA: Stanford University Press.

Leneman, L. (1991) *A Guid Cause: the Women's Suffrage Movement in Scotland*. Aberdeen: Aberdeen University Press.

Leneman, L. (1998) 'A truly national movement: the view from outside London', in M. Joannou and J. Purvis (eds), *The Women's Suffrage Movement: New Feminist Perspectives*. Manchester: Manchester University Press.

Levine, P. (1987) *Victorian Feminism 1850–1900*. Hutchinson.

Levine, P. (1990) *Feminist Lives in Victorian England*. Oxford: Blackwell.

Liddington, J. (2006) *Rebel Girls: Their Fight for the Vote*. Virago.

Liddington, J. and Norris, J. (1978) *One Hand Tied Behind Us: The Rise of the Women's Suffrage Movement*. Virago.

LNSWS Executive Committee minutes, 26 July 1926. Women's Library.

Lovenduski, J., Norris, P. and Burness, C. (1994) 'The party and women', in A. Seldon and S. Ball (eds), *Conservative Century*. Oxford: Oxford University Press.

Marcus, J. (ed.) (1987) *Suffrage and the Pankhursts*. Routledge.

Marwick, A. (1977) *Women at War 1914–1918*. Croom Helm.

Mason, F. (1986) 'The newer Eve: the Catholic Women's Suffrage Society in England, 1911–1923', *Catholic Historical Review*, 72, pp. 620–38.

Mayhall, L. (2003) *The Militant Suffrage Movement: Citizenship and Resistance in Britain, 1860–1930*. New York: Oxford University Press.

McCrillis, N. (1998) *The Conservative Party in the Age of Universal Suffrage*. Columbus: Ohio State University Press.

Melman, B. (1988) *Women and the Popular Imagination in the Twenties*. Macmillan.

Mitchell, H. (1977) *The Hard Way Up*. Virago.

Montefiore, D. (1927) *From a Victorian to a Modern*. E. Archer.

Morgan, D. (1975) *Suffragists and Liberals: the Politics of Woman Suffrage in Britain*. Oxford: Blackwell.

Mulvihill, M. (1989) *Charlotte Despard*. Pandora.

NUSEC *Annual Report 1928–1929*, p. 3.

NUSEC Executive Committee minutes, 24 May 1927. Women's Library, box 341, 2/nusec/A1/5 (7).

Pankhurst, C. (1959) *Unshackled: The Story of How We Won the Vote*. Hutchinson.

Pankhurst, S. (1977) *The Suffragette Movement*. Virago; orig. pub. 1931.

Pedersen, S. (2004) *Eleanor Rathbone and the Politics of Conscience*. New Haven, CT: Yale University Press.

Pugh, M. (1978) *Electoral Reform in War and Peace 1906–18*. Routledge.

Pugh, M. (1985) *The Tories and the People 1880–1935*. Oxford: Blackwell.

Pugh, M. (1992) *Women and the Women's Movement in Britain 1914–1959*. Macmillan.

Pugh, M. (2000) *The March of the Women: A Revisionist Account of the Campaign for Women's Suffrage, 1866–1914*. Oxford: Oxford University Press.

Pugh, M. (2001) *The Pankhursts*. Penguin.

Purvis, J. (1998) 'Christabel Pankhurst and the Women's Social and Political Union', in M. Joannau and J. Purvis (eds), *The Women's Suffrage Movement: New Feminist Perspectives*. Manchester: Manchester University Press.

Purvis, J. (2002) *Emmeline Pankhurst: A Biography*. Routledge.

Purvis, J. and Holton, S. (eds) (2000) *Votes for Women*. Routledge.

Ramsden, J. (1978) *The Age of Balfour and Baldwin 1902–40*. Longman.

Rasmussen, J. (1984) 'Women in Labour: the flapper vote and party system transformation in Britain', *Electoral Studies*, 3, pp. 47–63.

Rathbone, E. (1936) 'Changes in Public Life', in R. Strachey (ed.), *Our Freedom and Its Results*. Hogarth Press.

Rendall, J. (2001) 'John Stuart Mill, Liberal politics, and the movements for women's suffrage', in A. Vickery (ed.), *Women, Privilege, and Power: British Politics, 1750 to the Present*. Stanford, CA: Stanford University Press.

'Report of the SJC for 1920–21', *Labour Woman*, June 1921, p. 100.

Romero, P. (1987) *E. Sylvia Pankhurst: Portrait of a Radical*. New Haven, CT: Yale University Press.

Rosen, A. (1974) *Rise Up, Women! The Militant Campaign of the Women's Social and Political Union 1903–1914*. Routledge.

Rover, C. (1967) *Women's Suffrage and Party Politics in Britain, 1866–1914*. Routledge.

Rubinstein, D. (1986) *Before the Suffragettes: Women's Emancipation in the 1890s*. Brighton: Harvester Press.

Rubinstein, D. (1991) *A Different World For Women: The Life of Millicent Garrett Fawcett*. Brighton: Harvester Press.

Scott, S. (1998) *Feminism and the Politics of Working Women: The Women's Co-operative Guild, 1880s to the Second World War*. UCL Press.

Seldon, A. and Ball, S. (eds) (1994) *Conservative Century: The Conservative Party since 1900*. Oxford: Oxford University Press.

Shepherd, J. (2002) *George Lansbury: At the Heart of Old Labour*. Oxford: Oxford University Press.

Smith, H. (1984) 'Sex vs. class: British feminists and the Labour movement, 1919–1929', *The Historian* [US], 47, pp. 19–37.

Smith, H. (1990) 'British feminism in the 1920s', in H. L. Smith (ed.), *British Feminism in the Twentieth Century*. Aldershot: Edward Elgar.

Smith, H. (1992) 'The politics of Conservative reform: the equal pay for equal work issue, 1945–1955', *Historical Journal*, 35:2, pp. 401–15.

Stanley, L. and Morley, A. (1988) *The Life and Death of Emily Wilding Davison*. The Women's Press.

Stocks, M. (1949) *Eleanor Rathbone*. Gollancz.

Strachey, R. (1988) *The Cause: A Short History of the Women's Movement in Britain*. Virago; orig. pub. 1928.

Swanwick, H. (1935) *I Have Been Young*. Gollancz.

Tanner, D. (1990) *Political Change and the Labour Party 1900–1918*. Cambridge: Cambridge University Press.

Thane, P. (2001) 'What difference did the vote make?' in A. Vickery (ed.), *Women, Privilege, and Power: British Politics, 1750 to the Present*. Stanford, CA: Stanford University Press.

Thompson, W. and Wheeler, A. (1983) *An Appeal of One Half the Human Race. . . .* Virago; orig. pub. 1825.

Tickner, L. (1988) *The Spectacle of Women: Imagery of the Suffrage Campaign 1907–14*. Chatto and Windus.

Turner, J. (1992) *British Politics and the Great War*. New Haven, CT: Yale University Press.

Tusan, M. (2005) *Women Making News: Gender and the Women's Periodical Press in Britain*. Urbana: University of Illinois Press.

Ugolini, L. (2000) '"It is only justice to grant women's suffrage": Independent Labour Party men and women's suffrage, 1893–1905', in C. Eustance, J. Ryan and L. Ugolini (eds), *A Suffrage Reader: Charting Directions in British Suffrage History*. Leicester: Leicester University Press.

van Wingerden, S. (1999) *The Women's Suffrage Movement in Britain, 1866–1928*. Macmillan.

Vellacott, J. (1993) *From Liberal to Labour with Women's Suffrage: The Story of Catherine Marshall*. Montreal: McGill-Queen's University Press.

'Waging the sex war', *Woman's Leader*, 29 April 1927, p. 95.

Walker, L. (1984) 'Party political women: a comparative study of Liberal women and the Primrose League', in J. Rendell (ed.), *Equal or Different: Women's Politics 1800–1914*. Oxford: Basil Blackwell.

Walkowitz, J. (1980) *Prostitution and Victorian Society: Women, Class, and the State*. Cambridge: Cambridge University Press.

Wiltsher, A. (1985) *Most Dangerous Women: Feminist Peace Campaigners of the Great War*. Pandora.

Winslow, B. (1996) *Sylvia Pankhurst: Sexual Politics and Political Activism*. UCL Press.

'Women Unionists and Franchise', *The Times*, 27 May 1927, p. 13.

Index